CHAS

Creative & Editorial Direction
AllRightsReserved

Associate Producer
Janet Lui (AllRightsReserved)

Contributing Editor
Taka Nakanishi

Japanese Coordinator
Etsuko Yoshizawa

Copywriter
Cherise Fong

Art Director
AllRightsReserved, Godfrey Kwan (junkie design)

Designer
Godfrey Kwan (junkie design)

Photographer
Myke Cheng

First Published in 2007 by AllRightsReserved Ltd.
tel: (852) 2712 0873
fax: (852) 2712 6701
url: www.allrights-reserved.com

For General Enquires: info@allrights-reserved.com
For Distribution: garylau@allrights-reserved.com
For Editorial Submission & Collaborations
editor@allrights-reserved.com

ISBN 978-988-99001-5-1

SUPER PREMIUM

SOME CALL THEM FREEBIES, SOME SAY IT'S PRIVILEGE, SOME LIKE IT FANCY, SOME WANT IT HANDY. THERE MAY BE NO ONE DEFINITION FOR THE MULTITUDE OF NOVELTY GADGETS, BUT THEY ALL SHARE A COMMON GOAL - TO MAKE US REMEMBER. BIG OR SMALL, HANDED OUT IN PUBLIC OR PRESENTED ON RSVP, THESE PRICELESS PRODUCTS POPULATE OUR LIFESTYLES. LET'S WANDER THROUGH THE WONDERFUL WORLD OF SUPER PREMIUM.

*Pro***logue**

What does "premium" mean to you? Is it that coveted prize, that extra service, that token of thanks, that collectible party favor? Is it simply that little toy at the bottom of the cereal box that makes it all worth it? Or is it that priceless VIP gift that makes an unforgettable impression?

In applying different means to a common end - brand recognition - five makers and shakers share with us a wide range of "premium" interpretations. On the popular end of the spectrum, Japanese network corporation Docomo describes the "mushroom effect" of starting an expandable family of friendly characters to gain customers' trust. On the high end, French lifestyle boutique colette offers her clientele a taste of chic and a sense of clique with exclusive, curated, catered events - with just a hint of spontaneity and surprise.

But for most of us, the premium is that tangible object of desire, that limited-edition collector's item that we feel privileged to own. A premium not only promotes the brand, it makes the receiver feel special. As the commissioner and designer of one of the first commercial premium series in 1937, the traditional Japanese cosmetics company Shiseido makes its motive clear: "To express our appreciation to our customers."

Today, premium gifts are not just for the ladies who lunch. Trendy freebies and grab-bag gadgets can be used to promote anything from a new store opening to an upcoming movie release, while a clever collectible may be just what it takes to raise awareness of a social cause.

Still, each premium is a standalone work of promotional design. Whether it be a perishable dark chocolate invitation to a Fall-Winter fashion show or a post-production studio's souvenir tube of ping-pong balls, the receiver may always find pleasure in the object itself.

This book proposes a visual panorama of exceptional premium designs for all occasions. From the hallmark sealing stamp of your own initial to the retro Viewmaster slide of rotating fashion patterns, the super premium is that special gift that you'll never forget.

cd.	creative director/	c.	copywriter	f.	design firm/ agency
	executive creative director	ph.	photographer	cl.	client
ad.	art director	t.	typographer	m.	manufacture/ printer
d.	designer	at.	artist	p.	publisher
i.	illustrator	ch.	character design	y.	year of production
a.	author	pl.	planner		

shop opening   fashion show   new shop/company   exhibition   advertising   anniversary   product launch   branding   movie   by collectors

PartA MeetTheMakers

Extraordinary premium for promoting your brand

WHAT MAKES A GOOD MEMENTO? PRACTICALITY? LUXURY? GIMMICK? OR JUST PLAIN SINCERITY?
FROM THE ONES WHO MAKE IT HAPPEN TO THE ONES WHO RECEIVE THE COMPLIMENTS, WHAT
GOES ON BEHIND THE SCENES? TWO BRANDS, AN EVENT PLANNER AND A FASHION SOCIALITE
OFFER THEIR INDIVIDUAL POINTS OF VIEW ON THIS PROTEAN PLATFORM FOR BRANDING.

*Culture Beauty*InterviewWithShiseido

Founded well over a century ago, Shiseido stays true to its traditional Japanese roots and customs, while persevering in its mission to incorporate Western knowledge, ideas and trends. The company's cultural activities focus on preservation and exhibitions, as well as support and contribution to social welfare and the arts.

Hand-painted powder case, 1959

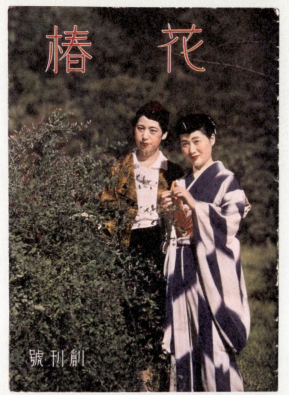

1st issue of Hanatsubaki, 1937

Shiseido Monthly News, 1928

Would you please introduce Shiseido?
Shiseido was established in 1872 in Ginza, Tokyo, as the first pharmacy of Western medicine in Japan. It began by producing and distributing cosmetics based on Western medicine prescriptions. One of Shiseido's first products, Eudermine skin lotion, has been on the market ever since.

What is Hanatsubaki-kai?
Hanatsubaki-kai is a members-only club for loyal Shiseido customers, founded in 1937 to offer make-up tips and cultural information for modern ladies. Today Hanatsubaki-kai counts around 9 million members, while special events include the annual Hanatsubaki-kai gathering, plus exclusive beauty lectures and fashion shows.

How did Hanatsubaki magazine begin?
The first issue of "Hanatsubaki" magazine was issued in November, 1937, especially for the establishment of Hanatsubaki-kai. It took over in-house magazines "Shiseido Monthly News" (1924-1930) and "Shiseido Graph" (1933-1937). Still published every month, Shiseido's free Hanatsubaki magazine offers articles on domestic and overseas fashion, travel and the arts.

What kinds of premiums were offered exclusively to Hanatsubaki-kai members?
We have made more than a thousand different premiums over the years. The first premium offered to members who bought a certain amount of Shiseido products was the Vanity Case in 1937. The other classic premiums are the Nishijin-Ori (traditional textile) handbag in 1938 and the Ceramic Sash Clip in 1939. All of them are made as gifts to express our appreciation to our customers, as well as an expression of our own aesthetic.

Shiseido Graph, 1933

Vanity case, 1937
After the Meiji Restoration in the 19th century,
Japanese culture and lifestyle were highly influenced
by Westernization. This influence also extended to
premium gift design: this vanity case includes not only
mini-size cosmetics, but a handy cigarette clip for
daily use.

Lucky straw sandals, 1933

Nishijin-Ori Handbag – exclusively for Hanatsubaki Club members, 1938

Why do all these premiums present such a strong Japanese style?
In the early period of the Showa era (1920's-1930's), 90 percent of Japanese women still wore kimonos and traditional clothing. During the first few years of Hanatsubaki-kai, manufacturers were forced to make products with very limited materials, given the economic constraints of the war. So they looked around many production districts and factories and tried hard to create something using both traditional methods and new techniques. Finally they produced a lot of Japanese-style goods. Today we still have much appreciation for precious Japanese traditional crafts, so we select works by artists who have a good relationship with Shiseido.

What was Shiseido's original design concept?
The Shiseido tradition of excellence in design and advertising can be traced back to its first president Shinzo Fukuhara, the son of founder Arinobu Fukuhara. Years of travel and study in the United States and Europe left a lasting impression on Shinzo which was to later be expressed as an aesthetic approach to product design and advertising never before seen in Japan.
After studying in the United States, from 1908 Shinzo traveled to France, where he took approximately 2,000 photographs. Shinzo's interest in photography was supported by theory, and he even formed the "Shashin-Geijyutsu-sha" to issue periodicals dealing with photographic theory and photography as an art.
In 1916, Shinzo established a design department and hired staff to work exclusively with advertising and its creation, despite the fact that Shiseido only had one cosmetics store at the time. The team of gifted young artists broke new ground in both product design and advertising. Design focused on art nouveau styles with touches of art deco and use of the arabesque. This creative interpretation of refined European designs gradually grew into what can be called a unique "Shiseido Style". Shinzo Fukuhara believed everything "must be rich" and that "the product should speak for itself". This philosophy guides Shiseido product formulation and creativity to this day.
* Courtesy of Shiseido Corporate Museum

Poster for Shiseido Cosmetics, promoted novelty lucky straw sandals, 1933

In the early stage (1920-1930), Shiseido was Japan's only private Western-style pharmacy, when herbal medicine was still mainstream. To reflect its avant-garde image, Shiseido made premium souvenirs influenced by Western art-deco style.

Contemporary, clean and highly-functional members' premiums were conceived and produced in the 1960s, as Japan developed into a modern society. As people paid more attention to their personal appearance, souvenirs became cosmetic cases, handbags and sewing kits.

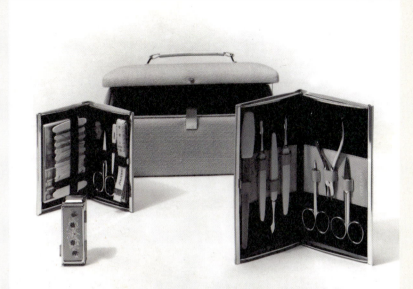

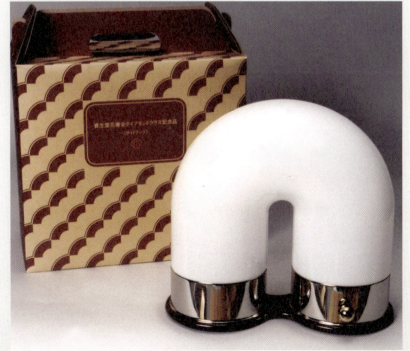

Shiseido's successful industrialization allowed for electric, and often mass-produced, novelty goods. By the late 1960s to '80s, many souvenirs had evolved from handy beauty accessories to daily household items.

Wordplay×Amusement×LifeStyle
StoryOfDocomodake

Docomodake mushroomed from the pioneering Japanese mobile-communications company NTT DoCoMo, as a promotional character to renew their brand image. But what began as a cute mascot finally sparked a family-oriented fad in all kinds of media and premium goods. Established in 1992, NTT DoCoMo has one of the largest subscriber bases of any mobile-phone company in the world.

A set of three stuffed Docomodake (Dad, Mom and Son)

Final sketch - the mushroom as new character

How did Docomodake come into being?

Docomodake was born in January 2005, originally to accompany the launch of the family-discount campaign. At that time, NTT DoCoMo had the image of a brand with expensive service charges. To optimize our service plan for families with two or more DoCoMo mobile phones, we launched Family Discount, which allowed families to carry over two months the remaining free communication fee, while the leftover talk-time could be shared among the family. We also offered free text messaging among families members, a service which was provided only by NTT DoCoMo at the time.

We came up with some ideas to promote the service, but none of them were convincing. On one hand we wanted to emphasize the exclusive service that only DoCoMo could provide, but on the other hand we believed that the advertising department should always adopt the customers' point of view. How would we appeal to people in a charming way? We were stuck. The mushroom we named Docomodake was born from this desperate situation.

ムービースター
ドコモダケ、現わる。

NTT
Do Co Mo

Advertising main visuals for "Press Conference again"

Why a mushroom called Docomodake?

"dake" is a play on word, which in Japanese means both "only" or "exclusive" and "mushroom" or "fungus". The first Docomodake drawing did not look cute. The next one was cute but not enough to gain people. At this point in the discussion, I made a quick sketch. Later, the ad agency created the Docomodake character based on my drawing, which we all liked perfectly.

Docomodake's charm lies in its widely spaced eyes, staring vacantly, and the "X" at each end of its mouth, to prevent it from boasting or even speaking. Thus we finally achieved a quiet and strange, but very attractive character, with a special presence. So we put it to work at once to launch the Family Discount campaign. The first TV commercial announced Docomodake at the press conference with family-friendly images to call attention to the "family = Docomodake" connection.

How did people react?

To tell the truth, the in-house response was not at all good. They saw the Docomodake character as a silly joke. Pressure from in-house colleagues was really tough.

How did Docomodake's reputation improve?

Even after the first draft of the character, I already felt we should make a stuffed Docomodake our official mascot. Unlike the sales department, we in the publicity department do not usually communicate with our customers directly, so we don't produce any novelty goods. However, I decided to create a set of three stuffed Docomodake (Dad, Mom and Son) on our own. About two weeks after the TV commercial began airing, the bosses in the company who had first given us bitter comments on Docomodake asked us if there were any Docomodake goods or gifts. That was the trigger. Surprising reactions from customers such as these finally called for the sales department's participation in this project.

So customers loved Docomodake from the start?

Right. It became such a boom that we created sequels to the TV commercial series. We kept updating new commercials almost every month. Strangely, however, we feel anxiety when something becomes so popular, as if the Docomodake bubble will burst and people will get bored quickly. So we made Docomodake appear as a secondary

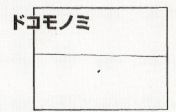

The Japanese words for "flea" and "deer"
also contain the word for "only"

ジュニアもシニアも、
ワイドなしあわせ。

中学生以下と60歳以上の方へ。「ファミ割ワイド」で、基本使用料が、月々1,575円(税込)。

Premium gift designs are always associated directly with the visuals of the current campaign. For the second phase of the promotion targeting teenagers and senior citizens, the main visuals were family members pinicking together in the woods. In order to keep the momentum of the campaign, Docomo produced thematic novelty items such as picnic cloths, lunchboxes, cups and plates, as well outdoor balls and plush toys.

あまった無料通信分を2ヶ月くりこしたあと、
通話代やパケット代としても
家族でわけあえるから、いいんだよー。

※「ファミリー割引」はお申込みが必要です。※お申込みの翌月から割引適用となります。※2ヶ月くりこし後のあまった無料通信分が家族でわけあえます。

ファミリー 割引

www.nttdocomo.co.jp/

優先席付近では、携帯電話の電源をお切りください。また、それ以外の場所では、マナーモードに切替え、通話はご遠慮願います。

NTT Do Co Mo

家族どうしの長文メール、
FOMAならデコメールも、
送受信無料で、いいんだよー。

新 いちねん 割引 + ファミリー 割引 = 基本使用料 最大50%OFF
最大25%OFF　25%OFF　継続利用期間が10年超の場合

※FOMA対応機種による10,000バイトより大きい画像自動受信(iモードメール2MB対応機種の場合は100KB)および、movaのiショット送受信など、一部無料とならないメールがあります。

Advertising posters hung in a train promoting the family mail discount, May 2005

character in the 4th and 5th promotions, to avoid media overexposure. After a while, we highlighted it in "Press Conference again" in September. All this time we strived to keep the campaign alive so that people would not get bored of the Docomodake story.

How much control did you have over the character's image and development?
In addition to story development, we were especially attentive to its visual approach - beginning with the stuffed Docomodake, animation, CG, and its various other incarnations, such as "Art Docomodake" by CG artist Ichiro Tanida. Docomodake was represented not only on flat surfaces, but also in complex media such as CD, picture book, or 3-D figures. It was so exciting when we made "Docomodake House", people were really surprised. There are a lot of gimmicks in the story, too. For example, they turn upside-down when going into the water. Many customers enjoy such gimmicks, which are always hot topics on the website, just like RPG. The point is that we made a special effort to "keep it fresh".

How has the Docomodake family itself mushroomed since the beginning?
In the second period of the campaign, we expanded the range of our discount service to seniors and junior-high students, so we made Grandpa, Grandma and brothers. The next year, Daughter, who lived away from her family, was created, to show that the discount service could also apply to people who live alone. Thus, we expanded the Docomodake

story. So as not to devalue it, we maintain a strict control over licensing, just like for a celebrity. We also selected third parties to collaborate in product development very carefully.

Which character is the latest addition to the Docomodake family?
"Kareshi-Docomodake", Boyfriend of Daughter. So far newly introduced characters have been associated with the service, but Boyfriend is the first one to have nothing to do with it. Hereafter, it may happen that Boyfriend gets married with Daughter and their baby is born. That way, the story still has a long way to go!

What kinds of Docomodake novelty goods have you created so far?
As of March, 2007, we have 251 different kinds of novelty items. At first we controlled them pretty tightly, but we later opened up a bit, as we saw Docomodake become more established as a popular character. Some unique items can fetch high prices on Internet auction sites. 36 million Docomodake mobile-phone cleaners and stuffed characters, as well as more than 12.6 million straps have been produced in total.

What does Docomodake have in store for the future of the mushroom family?
We hope the campaign will last as long as possible, as Docomodake is now an integral character of the company. Yet we would also like to maintain and upgrade its "value".

Making customers happy and making ourselves happy. Docomodake is a character originally created to bring families closer together. In a broader perspective, it can be seen as the character of love for all humankind, making good friends with everyone. It might sound ambitious, but we would like to raise it to the symbol of world peace. Actually NTT DoCoMo is a corporation consisting of nine separate companies, and until a few years ago each company created its own TV commercial. At the time we tried to integrate these companies as much as possible, following corporate policy. Since the birth of Docomodake, it has been a common character for sales promotion in all companies, and has also provided us with a means to identify each other. As a result, we ourselves have succeeded in establishing a good relationship with each other as one corporation!

Another perspective is overseas development. NTT DoCoMo has many offices all over the world, and receives a lot of overseas inquiries about Docomodake. It would be great if Docomodake gains the international reputation of someone like Takashi Murakami, a famous Japanese artist who is also highly praised overseas.

Which souvenir items are most special to you personally today?
The set of three stuffed Docomodake, Dad, Mom and Son. It was a high-stakes gamble to make them, as it was at the very beginning of the whole Docomodake movement. It is still deeply moving to see them even now.

❶

❶ *Playing cards using Docomodake family members
as the four suits.*
❷ *Hot-spring bathing salt and bathroom set for
Spring 2006 Family Discount campaign.*
❸ *Docomodake reusable puzzle calendar.*

❷

❸

⚘ *New Year special Docomodake doll set in the motif of Shichi Fukujin (Seven Gods of Fortune) in a box with Takarabun e (Treasure Ship) background. The Japanese tradition holds that the seven gods will arrive on the New Year and distribute fantastic gifts and good fortune.*

⚘ *Print advertisements using Daughter who lives alone, to promote phone mail discount for remote family mambers.*

⚘⚘ *Catering to all the needs of each family member, golf ball gift sets and member pins are offered to fathers who can enjoy the cute Docomodake faces a they tee off on the green.*

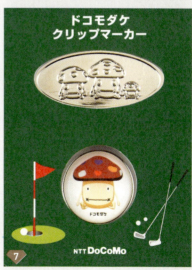

Interview courtesy of
NTT DoCoMo, Inc.
Director of Advertising group
Advertisement Department
Corporate Branding Division
Masato Kabasawa

StyleDesignArtFood
InterviewWithColette

*For colette, "premium" refers not to a promotional object, but
to an exceptional event, resulting in an unforgettable experience. Situated
in the heart of Paris, colette's multi-level boutique retails, exhibits and serves
"styledesignartfood" in trendsetting fashion, while the brand curates, hosts
and organizes ever-surprising "premium" events.*

©KUNTZEL+DEYGAS

Invitation to the 10th anniversary dinner

What does "premium" mean to you?
Exclusivity - Quality - Limited production -
Unexpected. A "premium" event requires the
skillful mix of a unique place, great music
and live performance, the right guests... and
perfect catering. But be careful to not "try
too hard", because when it's too controlled,
too sophisticated, you can lose its natural energy and all the spontaneous little things that
make an event unique.

*Which of the many "premium" events, exhibitions
and fashion shows you have attended over the
years were the most impressive?*
The Louis Vuitton party inside a bubble built
for the event in a park in Tokyo. The recent
Chanel show at Santa Monica airport, even if
I was not there. Our 10th anniversary dinner
party. For exhibitions, I think of the actual
"Wrong Store" in NYC. For fashion shows,
many from Alexander McQueen, Hussein
Chalayan, Comme des Garçons...

Your most memorable experience?
I'm very sorry to be ego-concerned, but I can
only think of the event we did in 2002, inviting
400 people to take a special train to Ghent
in Belgium for an all-night party at the new
Culture Club, with a lineup including 2Many-
Dj's, James Murphy, etc.

COLETTE N°4 CELEBRATION
COLETTE GOES TO CULTURE CLUB
AFRIKALAAN 174 9000 GENT
JOIN US AT 9PM
SAMEDI 26 OCTOBRE
TO DIMANCHE 27 OCTOBRE 2002
PARTY ALL NIGHT
**WITH 2 MANY DJ S, THE RAPTURE,
VIVE LA FETE, LCD SOUND SYSTEM,
TREVOR JACKSON, SCISSOR SISTERS, PRANCE...**
PARISIANS COMING AT 10 PM
INFO : IPARTY@COLETTE.FR / (33) 1 42 61 74 46
THIS INVITATION IS PERSONAL AND REQUESTED AT THE DOOR.

colette goes to culture club, Belgium 2002

©KUNTZEL+DEYGAS

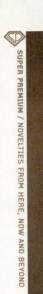

©KUNTZEL+DEYGAS

Which of your own curated events and exhibitions would you rank among your top five?

In addition to the two already mentioned: Exhibition UK Jack, OK !, March 2006; colette dance class "Around the World" in Tokyo, summer 2006; our party in 2000 at the Palais de Chaillot, in front of the Eiffel Tower, with minimix and the party at Opera Garnier with Visionaire in 1999; our 5th anniversary party with Crazy Horse dancers in the basement; Caperino & Peperone (Kuntzel+Deygas), many collaborations.

What inspires these exceptional events?

For us, premium events result from a natural search for quality, for mixing talents. They're not events limited to 50 super VIPs. They're more open, but produced with lots of attention to every detail. We need this medium to express our belief that colette is not limited to being just another retail store. colette is more... and wants to give you always more. We get our inspiration from meeting people, from visiting spaces, and from going to other premium events!

What differences do you see in various events around the world?

Differences can come from the location's access and from the city's rules... But today, there are fewer and fewer differences, I'm afraid, as everything is so internationally global, thanks to the Internet.

What "premium" trends do you anticipate in the future?

I guess to surprise more and more, to push the limits – to spend more and more money, too! Maybe to explore some new countries. Maybe to stay at home and enjoy virtual events, while ghosts come to you. (I was very impressed with all the new light and projection techniques at Justin Timberlake's show!)

Can you tell us about colette's 10th anniversary celebration?

We invited 180 guests right in front of the colette shop. They were surprised to walk just a little to discover the Hotel Saint-James right next to us, a beautiful old hotel particulier, which we lit in blue and where we hosted a dinner with exclusive desserts on a great menu. We had a playlist by Michel Gaubert and introduced a video for the new song by the French band The Shoppings about "1997-2007" featuring Jeremy Scott. Then we joined the party at La Scala, a very classic '70s club, with more than 2,000 people. We had a lineup with the 10 best partymakers from the last 10 years in Paris. It was crazy and very exciting.

What would you like to attempt in the future?

Well, I prefer to not attempt anything and to be surprised!

In celebration of colette's 10th anniversary, Caperino & Peperone leapt across boundaries and left their marks on Lacoste polos and sneakers ♥ , Medicom Toy Be@rbricks, Linda Farrow vintage sunglasses, Goyard portfolio ♥ , Cartier "Marcelo" bags ♥ , and more. All these crossover projects take place around the globe, just as colette has ridden the winds of fashion over the past decade.

©KUNTZEL+DEYGAS

1

©KUNTZEL+DEYGAS

2 3

Playfully adolescent Caperino & Peperone help countdown the years to colette's 10th anniversary. Their designers Olivier Knutzel and Florence Deygas drew them into the numbers 1 to 10 as the main visuals of the anniversary campaign, including window displays and other collaborative birthday party favors.

10

1 2 3 4 5 6 7 8 9 10

©KUNTZEL+DEYGAS

SpecialBeautifulOrPractical
InterviewWithWinifredLai

Winifred Lai is a cross-media creative actively involved in fashion, editorial, advertising and information technology. Now a popular magazine columnist who travels around the world, she expresses her unique views on brands, fashion, lifestyle and other trendy disciplines of knowledge.

1

2

What does "premium" mean to you?
I could never figure out what this word really means. Something special, I suppose.

What was the very first premium souvenir you received?
Well, I got a lace-covered limited edition of Madonna's *Vogue* single. In fact, it was an internal copy from inside Warner Music. Someone who worked there who admired me very much gave it to me. Of course I like it very much!

Which of the many premium events, exhibitions and fashion shows you have attended over the years were the most impressive?
Hermes gave us a transparent Kelly Bag in October 1995, because there was a terrorist bombing in Paris, and the bag check in front of the show entrance took forever. So a transparent handbag was supposed to save some trouble.
Chanel gave out thermal pots and blankets (2006) as show souvenirs.
Jean-Paul Gaultier launched his first perfume, and they sent me a wooden box, which was modeled after a folded easel. I don't know why and how was it relevant to JPG Parfum, but the box is very beautiful. I have kept it till now.
The "Casino Royale" premiere hosted by Omega. I did not win a watch, but I really like the Casino Royale playing cards they gave me, since I really love the relationship between James Bond and Vesper Lynd in the movie.

When you receive an impressive premium, how does it change your perception of this brand?
Oh, all those big bucks they made!

Which premiums from your personal collection would you rank among your top 5?
I don't rank them, because I did not collect them on purpose. But the ones I remember because they are so special are:
1. Hermes plastic rain head bonnet – only my grandmother or the Queen used something like that, and it reminds me of her
2. JPG Parfum wooden box (see Q3)
3. Chanel Key Chain – it's a new year's gift, it's really convenient because of the signature long chain
4. Chanel mobile chain – the miniature is beautiful, and everyone says so when they see it

3

4

5. Christian Dior and Comme des Garçons candles – I like things that I can use all the time ▼

What differences do you see in various events and their novelty goods around the world?
Japanese do it out of courtesy; Parisian big houses do it out of class; Hong Kong event organizers do it to attract more media.

In your opinion, what makes a good premium?
Special. Beautiful or Practical.

What "premium" trends do you anticipate in the future?
More and more brands and events will go out of their way to think of more special premiums, because it's highly competitive these days, even among premiums!

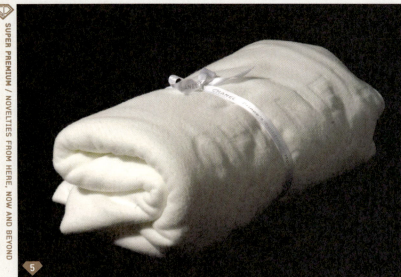

◆ *Chanel Haute Couture S/S 06 was unveiled at the re-opening of the Grand Palais in Paris, in the sub-freezing temperature of a crisp spring morning. Chanel offered its guests a white Chanel-branded blanket, accompanied by a trademark thermos of hot jasmine tea to keep them warm inside out.*

Originally known for its fine leather saddles, today Hermes is famous for its delicate silk scarves, first introduced in the 1930s, as well as its luxury leather goods, including the coveted Kelly and Birkin handbags. This foldable plastic rain bonnet, both practical and elegantly orange, is a premium gift for VIP guests.

8

Speaking of attention to detail among luxury brands, Chanel made miniatures of its classic icons – N°5 perfume, camellia and Eiffel Tower – and inlaid then into a thumb-sized mobile-phone strap ornament. Leaving nothing overlooked, Chanel reinforced the inside of its passport case with its own logo lining ◆, while Christian Dior uses cut-glass and gradient printing for the scented candle and glass. ◆ ◆

9

10

SUPER PREMIUM

FROM TRENDY TOKENS TO VIP GIFTS, FROM FRIENDLY FAMILY EVENTS TO SILKY SWANK SOIRÉES, A CELEBRATION IS ONLY AS MEMORABLE AS ITS NOVELTY SOUVENIR. SO WHAT'S GOOD? PRIVILEGE? SURPRISE? OPENING VIRAL PROMOTIONAL CHANNELS? SEE WHAT HAPPENS WHEN THE TRENDY DESIGNER TOY MEETS THE CENTURY-OLD LUXURY BRAND IN THIS SHOWCASE OF PREMIUM PRODUCTS.

PartBSeeThePremium

Extraordinary premium for your brand promotion

+41, 100% chocolate cafe.,
1LOVE, Agnes b.,
AllRightsReserved,
Ann Demeulemeester, Anna Sui,
Anteprima, Antoine+Manuel,
ARC worldwide, Art Village Osaki,
Atsuro Tayama, BEAMS, BUCCI,
Butterfly Stroke Inc., CHANEL,
Cibone, cocca, Diesel, Dunhill,
FLAME inc., Garcia Style, giraffe,
groovisions, hhstyle, Hello Kitty,
Kazunari Hattori, Maison Martin Margiela,
Maria Luisa, mint designs, Nike,
Naomi Hirabayashi, NTT DoCoMo,
offlohi, Omotesando Hills, Paperlux,
Paul & Joe, Ping Pong, Power Graphixx,
Sally Scott, Shanghai Tang, Shiseido,
Sunday Vision, Tsumori Chisato, Q-pot,
Uniqlo, Vivienne Westwood,
WABISABI, Young Kim

THIS EXCITING VISUAL PANORAMA OF NOVELTY GOODS FEATURES MEMENTOS FROM SHOP OPENINGS,
FASHION SHOWS, HOUSE WARMINGS, EXHIBITIONS, ADVERTISEMENTS, ANNIVERSARIES, MOVIE PREMIERES,
OR SIMPLY CORPORATE SOFT BRANDING. THE FOLLOWING PAGES OFFER A PREMIUM SELECTION OF FINE
PRODUCTS BY BOTH CREATORS AND COLLECTORS: INTRODUCING FASCINATING FREEBIES.

LOUIS VUITTON
2006·2007
FALL WINTER
SHOW WITH
MARC JACOBS

Louis Vuitton **FW0607**

Louis Vuitton's '80s-disco-themed F/W 0607 show with Marc Jacobs in Tokyo offered its 200 VIP guests a fashionable retro souvenir. The traditional Japanese toys, a kendama and three komas (spinning tops), are stamped with LV's playful branding to give guests a refreshing image of the East.

ad.   *Masayoshi Kodaira*
d.   *Masayoshi Kodaira*
f.   *FLAME, Inc.*
cl.   *LOUIS VUITTON*
y.   *2006*

 fashion show

*PolkaDots*Umbrella

Kusama's famous polka dots appear as wet water droplets on these brightly patterned umbrellas, available in two color combinations of red and white or yellow and black. Customers making purchases or donations to The Community Chest of Hong Kong can receive one polka-dot umbrella.

ad.   *AllRightsReserved*
a.   *Yayoi Kusama*
cl.   *Harbour City*
y.   *2007*

advertising
branding

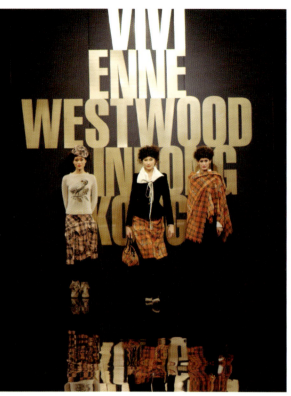

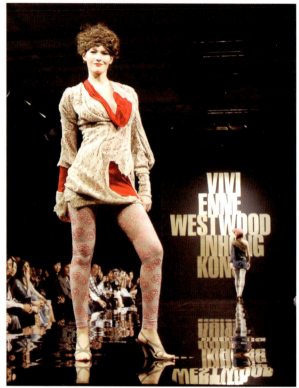

*Vivienne*Westwood

After rocking with British punk, Vivienne West-wood's F/W 0708 fashion show offers guests an elegant, delicate and peaceful souvenir: a gilded crystal snow ball music box.

f.   Vivienne Westwood
y.   2007

 fashion show

*Bape***GoldBrickTee**

Before the Earth became the Planet of the Apes, a hot spot next to Hong Kong's Landmark building was transformed into a crucial battlefield in 2006 AD. Thus marked the grand opening of the Bape Hong Kong flagship store on April 1st, driving Bape maniacs crazy. To prove it was no April Fool's joke, Bape die-hards each received a limited-edition A Bape Gold Brick containing a compressed tee, distributed exclusively at the Hong Kong opening.

f.   *A Bathing Ape, I.T*
y.   *2006*
✂   *shop opening*

Chanel 1000% **Bearbrick**

Since the launch of Medicom Toy's well-known Bearbrick, Chanel is the first luxury brand to create and exhibit it as an art piece in its stores. Designed by Karl Lagerfeld himself, the figure reflects Chanel's famous icons – Coco Chanel outfit, camelia in the hair, pearl necklace, black sunglasses – as yet another fitting tribute to the visionary creator that was Coco Chanel.

While urban culture considers city life as an open-air, working-class gallery, Chanel and Bearbrick fuse pop culture and haute couture to illustrate Coco's own quote: "There is no fashion if it does not go down to the street." Chanel 1000% Bearbrick figures were not only for sale, but also presented to close friends.

f.   CHANEL
y.   2006
♕   *branding*

Chanel**VIPGift**

Sporting a white Coco Chanel outfit and smart white hat, this miniature young lady with a haughty pose reflects Chanel's vivacious attitude. Subtly branded with signature double "c", the bijou key chain introduces a personable and playful expression of luxury fashion – available exclusively for VIP members and guests.

f.　　*CHANEL*

 branding

*IamExpensiv*SS07

Vivienne Westwood's Red Label offers ladies a look that is both sexy and elegant, fun and easy. To convey the collection's relaxed theme, the fashion show souvenir was a gift box in the shape of the season's crayon flower illustration, containing a pair of cozy cotton socks.

f.   *Vivienne Westwood*
y.   *2007*

fashion show

*Celine*FemmesBrandNovelty

Chic and practical, Celine brings sensual glamor to the modern woman. Ever-elegant, the souvenir gift for the opening of Celine's Hong Kong flagship store on Peking Road was a mini scented-wood fan with silk-screened pattern, hot-stamped silver logo on the handle and metal wrist chain – a handy accessory to welcome customers into the sophisticated new boutique.

f.   *Celine*
y.   *2004*

shop opening
by collectors

ChristianDiorFan

Dior's F/W 08 haute couture collection presented a splendid display of stunning color and exceptional fantasy: "An Extreme Bal des Artistes". Guests received a white wooden fan printed with images of royal Versailles and the collection's extravagant title.

f.   *Christian Dior*
y.   *2007*
     fashion show
★   *by collectors*

AnteprimaMobileStrap

In yet another successful case of miniature signature, Anteprima shrunk its authentic wire bag into the eye-pleasing size of a mobile strap charmcharm, which was offered to customers and VIPs to thank them for their continued support. The snow-white, furry ball is designed to clean the phone's screen, gently dusting off the dirt with a fluffy cottontail.

f.   *ANTEPRIMA*
♛   *branding*

*DriesVanNoten*Amber-plasticComb

As Dries Van Noten's A/W 0607 Men's Collection was inspired from Bryan Ferry's video "Let's Stick Together", so was the fashion-show souvenir. In the music video, Ferry combs his hair flawlessly, so a small, thin comb is the necessary tool for perfection. All the fashion mongrels rushing from show to show can now keep their hair neat with this handy personalized accessory.

f. *Dries Van Noten*
y. *2007*

▲ *fashion show*
★ *by collectors*

*Moschino*KeyRing

The ever-chic Moschino shows its sense of humor with an everlasting exotic gift, in the form of a long metallic red hot chili pepper key ring, with crystal inset. For all those girls who just wanna have fun, the Italian luxury designer is making fun with fashion, using both imaginative and irreverently sarcastic invention, directly inspired by curious food shapes.

f.   *Moschino*

 fashion show

★   *by collectors*

*TsumoriChisato***OwlTapeCentimeterScale**

No longer merely the symbol of Tsumori Chisato Collections, the owl now offers a measuring service. It can measure your body by simply stretching its wings around your vital parts. No matter what your measurements, it's print-heavy with a healthy dose of manga and bohemian cuteness to comfort you.

f.   *Tsumori Chisato*
y.   *2007*

fashion show

TSUMORI CHISATO

*Tsumori*ChisatoSS07

The S/S 07 season's bright summer motif of orange and gold polka dots was transferred onto various VIP tokens of Tsumori Chisato's S/S 07 fashion show. This year's colletion took its cue directly from the hot season with the designer's signature clear-cut, chic-sweet patterns. Featured novelties included a playful, casual tote bag and cute round cosmetic mirror in a discreet black pouch.

f.   *Tsumori Chisato*
y.   *2006*

fashion show

FLOW
VIKTO

BOMB
ROLF

Viktor&Rolf **FlowerbombCharmBracelet**

This fine and dainty silver-plated charm bracelet is a token of the Dutch duo's prosperity. Their Flowerbomb campaign included the debut hand-grenade design perfume bottle, black-red theme of the S/S 05 ready-to-wear collection, and a dedicated website. The aristocratic collectible's seven magic charms include Viktor & Rolf sealing wax logo, V, &, R and Flowerbomb perfume bottle for a miniature floral fantasy for all fashionistas.

f.   *Viktor & Rolf*
y.   *2005*
▶   *product launch*
★   *by collectors*

MMM/HongKong

For its first flagship store in Hong Kong, Maison Martin Margiela invited guests to be part of the opening by offering them a key to the reception and a trompe-l'oeil goblet. As each goblet is designed with a transparent glass ball at its base, only when the goblet is filled with clear water can guests clearly read the message: "happy hong kong martin margiela".

f.   Maison Martin Margiela
y.   2006

 new shop/company

MMM EitaroSohonpo

This limited-edition candy box set was inspired by Maison Martin Margiela's iconic circled-number fashion line, conceived and produced with famous old candy workshop Eitaro Sohonpo for Isetan's 120th anniversary. Packaged inside a long white cotton tote bag, it combines MMM's simplicity with a touch of oriental zen.

f. *Maison Martin Margiela*
y. *2007*
  anniversary

*MMM*Invitation

The luxurious invitation to Maison Martin Margiela's fashion show during Paris Fashion Week F/W 0708 was a genuine bar of dark chocolate, with all information printed on its illustrated white paper wrapper. The chocolate invitation packaging was designed to attract guests to either a refined avant-garde evening or fine gourmet food. On a chilly autumn night, the complimentary candy bar promised to offer guests a bitter-sweet energy charge for an unforgettable night.

f. *Maison Martin Margiela*
y. *2007*
   fashion show

*CasinoRoyale*PlayingCards

True to the on-screen face-off between James Bond and Vesper Lynd, this royal deck of casino playing cards recalls all the glamorous thrills of the Hollywood movie blockbuster – coming soon to a card table near you.

y.   *2006*
 advertising
movie

*ROCHAS*FlowerBrooch

This pink rose brooch was made especially for Maria Luisa's boutique opening, with each petal assembled separately by hand, making each piece unique. ROCHAS was one of the fashion labels featured in the grand opening, originally from Paris and designed by Olivier Theyskens, to welcome new customers with that extra delicate touch.

f.   *Maria Lusia*
y.   *2006*
new shop/company

*Bape*ExpressGoldCard

How extravagant is the bling-bling lifestyle of the billionaire golden boy? Bape offers a clue with its member's exclusive, serial-numbered Ape VIP gift - a thin, floppy mousepad made in the image of an American Express credit card bearing the brand's primate icon, characteristic camouflage print and current years of operation: 1993-2005. If "money is the message", Bape bank's slogan is far less human: "Ape shall never kill ape."

f.   *A Bathing Ape*
y.   *2006*

MAISON MARTIN MARGIELA
PRES ENTATION HOMME
P SENTATION HOMME
DRINTEMPS | ETE 200 ME 8
DU JEUDI 28 JUIN AU
IMANCHE 1ER JUILLET
007 de 10h00 à T
00 LES QUATRES JOUR
POUR RENDEZVOUS
TEL : 0144 536 320 S
163 RUE DE ST MAUR 75011 PARIS
WWW.MAISONMARTINMARGIELA.COM

MMM CD Invitation

How does one make reservations for Maison Martin Margiela's Présentation Homme S/S 08 fashion show? Easy, just listen to the trilingual English, Japanese and French words of the "One Hour Continuous Instruction Dhamma Salila – March 16, 1998" audio book, and book your seat. Details are on the envelope. What's more, if you have the patience to listen to an entire hour of ambient sound, you will be rewarded with a little surprise.

f.   *Maison Martin Margiela*
y.   *2007*
     fashion show
★   *by collectors*

ANTEPRIMA 15thAnniversaryDollsGift

Produced by Heroine, the same company that manufactured the Visionnaire toy figures, these seven-inch-tall dolls of twin sisters Caco and Cuco come finely accessoried, all the way down to their signature Anteprima gold and silver handbags. Art director Izumi Ogino designed a gold bikini set and classic Anteprima dress as changeable apparel for the girls, along with a mini wire handbag key ring and mobile-phone strap.

f.   *ANTEPRIMA*
y.   *2007*
◆   *anniversary*

*ANTEPRIMA*15thAnniversaryDollsGift

*Santastic!***NoveltyTowel**

Japanese manga artist Santa Inoue's Santastic! brand introduces vivacious figures based on his own comic characters. His latest high-profile pop brand novelty is packaged into a glittering gold brick, stamped with the artist's self-portrait and SARU – the name of the lead gang in his famous work "Tokyo Tribe". No sweat, unfold the bling-bling wrapper to uncover a compressed towel.

f.   *Santastic!*
y.   *2007*

♔   *branding*
★   *by collectors*

Chloe **Candle**

The lock and shape signified everything – it's Paddington, and it drove people crazy. As Vogue famously said: "We bet Sienna Miller has one." Unsurprisingly, it was sold out at a breakneck pace, and there's probably a waiting list as long as your arm to get it from most boutiques. Meanwhile, you can use the candle as a kind of substitute for love, which was given out at the time the must-have item was launched.

f.   *Chloe*
y.   *2006*

A.T AliceInWonderlandPack

Exploring the magical world of fantasy stories, A.T's S/S 07 collection used the antique serigraphy illustrations of Lewis Carroll's literary classic *Alice in Wonderland* for a commemorative range of T-shirts. Upon any tee purchase, customers receive the gilded White Rabbit tote bag as a special gift.

f.   A.T
y.   2007

▶ *product launch*

e.m. 10th Anniversary **Book**

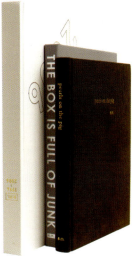

e.m.10thAnni. **Book**

To celebrate its 10th anniversary, e.m. chose
to bind a trio of books into one retrospective
album. Three volumes of past projects and
lush visuals add up to one decade of graphic
design nostalgia, in three distinct chapters:
"e.m. 1996-2006"; "pearls on the pig"; "THE
BOX IS FULL OF JUNK". The three-tiered anniversary album thus offers its fans three per-
spectives, 10 years, and a multitude of images
to remember e.m.

f.   *e.m.*
y.   *2007*

 anniversary

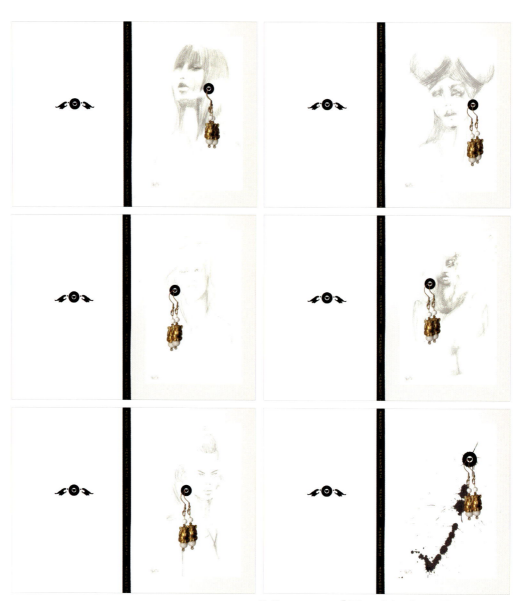

Meannorth **TuttiAnimali**

This gift was offered in conjunction with a limited-edition collection of prints from the Danish fashion label Meannorth. The designer decided to include a piece of artwork along with a pair of monkey earrings to complete the outfit, as well as to highlight the theme of the printed clothing, as all illustrations were created by the same designer.

ad. *Naja Conrad-Hansen*
i.   *Naja Conrad-Hansen*
cl. *Meannorth*
y.   *2006*

 branding

NHP06 *Meannorth**TuttiAnimali*

*Paul&Joe*CompanyGifts

Fashion and beauty label Paul & Joe revived their classic original patterns and illustrations to design this luxury box and deck of playing cards, presented to VIP members as a thank-you gift for their loyalty since the beginning of the brand named after the designer's two sons. Even the signature ace of spades contained the image of the loyal Siamese cat.

d.   Paul & Joe
f.   Paul & Joe
♔ *branding*

*Shanghai*ReduxCDInvitation

As the theme of Shanghai Tang's A/W 0607 collection was 1930s Shanghai nostalgia, souvenirs were a music CD and calendar-catalogue. Isabelle, the singer pictured on the CD jacket, recorded a remixed version of "Ye Lai Xiang", one of the classic Chinese songs of that era, and was one of the models in the calendar.

p.   *Eugenio Recuenco*
f.   *Shanghai Tang*
y.   *2007*
▶   *product launch*

*Pinceau*Christmas

Christmas paper freebies in the shape of reindeer, mistletoe and angels were delivered via post throughout the month of December as the brand's seasons' greetings. As each die-cut graphic is adorned with detailed gold foil hot stamp and embossing, they also make delicate ornaments on the Christmas tree.

ad.   *Naomi Hirabayashi*
d.   *Natsuko Yoneyama*
cl.   *Jun Co., Ltd.*
y.   *2006*

♛ *branding*

*YayoiKusama*PlayingCards

Avant-garde artist Yayoi Kusama's characteristic polka-dot patterns were used as the
visual theme of this artistic deck of playing
cards. Even the four suits of spades, hearts,
clubs and diamonds have all been reinterpreted, using fluorescent green, pink, blue and
red instead of the traditional red and black.

cd.   *Masayoshi Kodaira*
a.   *Yayoi Kusama*
cl.   *TAKEO Co., Ltd. / LOFT*
y.   *2007*

 exhibition

e.m. ChristmasGift2006

Accessory brand e.m. created the Christmas Express greetings especially for customers and members. Packaged as an express mail, a balloon was sent to customers along with a Christmas card and included straw to blow up the airy ornaments.

ad.   Masayoshi Tobita
d.   Tomoya Omori
i.   Tomoya Omori
ph.   Tomoya Omori
y.   2006

👑 *branding*

*GoldenChocolate***Bar**

This 400 percent golden chocolate brick is actually a cardboard box packed with tissues. To surprise customers at Q-pot's Harajuku shop opening, these gilded chocolate bars were handed to every guest and customer, in a tantalizingly delicious promotion of Q-pot's sweet-toothed theme.

d.   *Tadaaki Wakamatsu*
f.   *Q-pot*
y.   *2006*

✂   *shop opening*

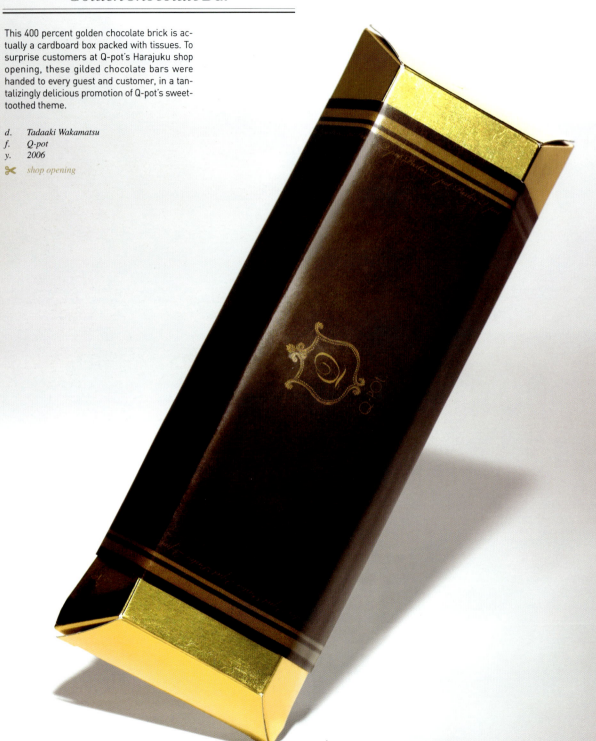

12MonthsOf SunAd

Sun Ad conceived their new year's greeting calendar with a set of 12 colored pencils, as they recall the first childhood tools of many advertising-agency creatives. Each month is matched to a specific color and elaborated into a phrase printed on the side of the box.

cl.   SUN AD
ad. Hiroshi Kichise
d.   Hiroshi Kichise
c.   Yasuhiko Sakura
y.   2005

 branding

"BUILD AND DESTROY" SERIES JIGSAW PUZZLE

Ref. Number:
00004
Manufacturer:

No of Pieces:
6
Dimensions:
8.7cm × 14cm / 3.42" × 5.51"
Puzzle Type:
Standard Jigsaws
Description:
A highly detailed puzzle with
a image of Mark II "Pineapple"
Grenade.
Suitable for age six and above.

© TAKEO PAPER SHOW 2007
ÉDIFICE × TAKEO
ART WORK: NOB
ART DIRECTION: NAOMI HIRABAYASHI

"THINK PEACE"

作っては壊すことを繰り返す
世界の破壊行動について、
もっと積極的に考えなければ。

"BUILD AND DESTROY" SERIES JIGSAW PUZZLE

© TAKEO PAPER SHOW 2007
ÉDIFICE × TAKEO
ART WORK: NOB
ART DIRECTION: NAOMI HIRABAYASHI

ThinkPeacePaperPuzzle

The "Build and Destroy" jigsaw set of five includes puzzles in the shape of a tank, machine gun, hand grenade, helmet and rocket. The anti-military message of the puzzles is simple: build weapons, destroy world peace. All puzzle pieces are made of colored cardboard. The "Think Peace" package was offered as a free gift to all purchasing customers.

ad.   Naomi Hirabayashi
i.   Nobuo Sekiguchi
cl.   Takeo Co., Ltd.
y.   2007
ⓒ exhibition

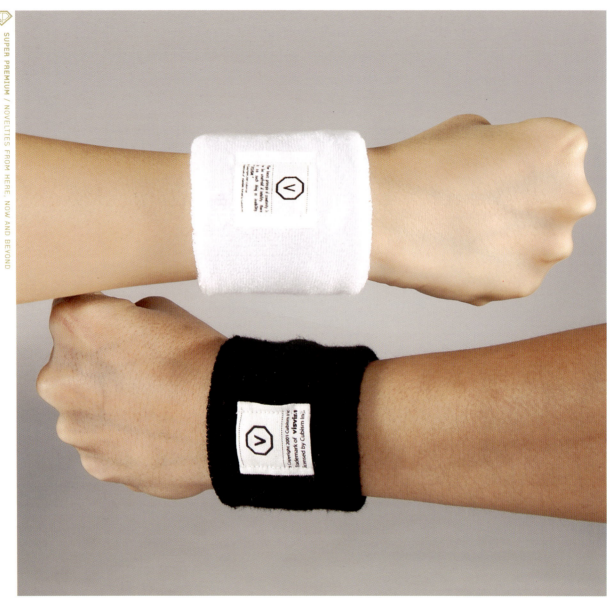

VISVIM F.I.LinHongKong

Japanese fashion label VISVIM was so-named after the clear-cut shapes of the letters used to spell it. This "clean" spirit is represented in their street apparel styles, which focus on quality over fancy appearance. For their first F.I.L (Free International Library) in Hong Kong, each guest received a pair of black and white wrist bands as a practical welcome gift.

f.   VISVIM
y.   2007

 shop opening

*300*SpartanHelmetPaperweight

"We are Spartans" said the legendary King Leonidas, in affirmation of his warriors' bravery and glory. This same essence is exhibited in the Spartan helmet, which Warner Bros. has reproduced in the form of a metal paperweight. The heroic symbolism exalted in the epic movie "300" now exerts its weight and power on paper instead of the Spartan head.

y.   2007

 movie

Special thanks to Warner Bros. Entertainment Inc

© 2007 SAKURAN Film Committe ©Moyoco Anno Kodansha

Reviving the atmosphere inhabited by courtesans of Japan's Edo period in vivid color, these Sakuran premiums combine the motifs of Moyoko Anno's original manga work with traditional Japanese patterns such as cherry blossoms, goldfish, chrysanthemums and butterflies. The accessories use wrapping cloth produced by kimono maker Kyoho, who also made the costumes used for the movie.

Posters and pressbook
ad.   Masayuki Tanijima, Emi Watanabe,
       Yoko Kawase (Asmic Ace)
d.   Tycoon Graphics
ph.   Mika Ninagawa

Wrapping cloth
ad.   Masayuki Tanijima, Emi Watanabe,
       Yoko Kawase (Asmic Ace)
d.   KYOHO inc.

Hair sticks
ad.   Yoshihiro Murata
d.   Ayumi Kobayashi
ph.   Miyako Kanno
y.   2006

Hand Mirror bag set
d.   Movic
i.   Moyoko Anno
y.   2007
⊗   *movie*

*Paris*JeT'aime

This omnibus movie of 18 short films about love in Paris by filmmakers from around the world called for an appropriately simple and universal design. Its premiere movie-screening premium reflects the sophisticated image of the French capital, reinterpreted as straight-forward streetwear for romantic ladies.

T-shirt & pin
d.   *IENA*
y.   *2007*

Poster
ad. *Osamu Oohashi (thumb M)*
d.   *Yuichi Ishii (thumb M)*
y.   *2007*
⊗   *movie*

© 2006 VICTOIRES INTERNATIONAL ET PIROL
FILM PRODUCTION

*Zooyork*Zoopreme

U.S. street-fashion brand and skateboard manufacturer Zooyork is known for both its wit and its Big Apple heritage. Its famously punny "Zoopreme" skateboard sticker was such a success among the public that Zooyork finally decided to produce a very limited quantity of Zoopreme skateboards as VIP premiums.

f.   *Zooyork*
y.   *2005*
♛   *branding*

*Ann*Demeulemeester

Every sketch starts with a single stroke. For her very first store to open in Hong Kong, Belgian fashion designer Ann Demeulemeester invited guests to create their own definition of fashion using this opening gift box of pencils.

f.   *Ann Demeulemeester*
y.   *2006*
✂   *shop opening*

*CdG*HongKong

As a souvenir of White Box, the flagship store of Comme des Garçons in Hong Kong's Central district, this clean and sophisticated square box contains a single white candle to light as a pure memento.

f.   *Comme des Garçons*
y.   *2006*
✂   *shop opening*

WE ARE HAPPY TO INVITE YOU TO
JOIN US CELEBRATE THE OPENING
OF COMME DES GARÇONS' WHITE BOX
IN HONG KONG

30 MARCH 2007

FROM 19:00

20 ON LAN STREET
CENTRAL,
HONG KONG

RSVP: GLORIA YU TEL: 852 2199 1902 / MAGGIE LEE TEL: 852 3107 1147

COMME des GARÇONS

COMME des GARÇONS
20 ON LAN STREET, CENTRAL, HONG KONG

WHITE BOX   COMME des GARÇONS

THE FIRST SHOP BY COMME DES GARÇONS IN HONG KONG IS OPENING ON 31 MARCH 2007. AFTER MORE THAN 25 YEARS OF DOING BUSINESS IN HONG KONG, COMME DES GARÇONS IS PROUD AND HAPPY TO FINALLY HAVE ITS OWN SHOP TO EXPRESS ITS SENSE OF VALUES IN A STRONG AND DIRECT WAY.

THE NEW STORE WILL CARRY AN EDITED MIX OF ALL COMME DES GARÇONS BRANDS AS WELL AS SPECIALS AND EXCLUSIVE ITEMS.

REI KAWAKUBO HAS ENVISIONED A WHITE BOX, A PURE AND MONOLITHIC STRUCTURE, THE COMME DES GARÇONS CASTLE. SHE LIKES THE IDEA OF PEOPLE ARRIVING AT THE CASTLE THROUGH ZETLAND STREET, THE WONDERFUL OLD HONG KONG MARKET STREET UP FROM QUEENS ROAD CENTRAL, AND INTO ON LAN STREET, JUXTAPOSING THE FEELING OF GOOD OLD HONG KONG WITH ULTRA MODERN HONG KONG.

CONCEPTION/DESIGN: REI KAWAKUBO
THIRD FLOOR DECOR: MICHAEL HOWELLS
GROUND FLOOR ARTWORK: YUICHI HIGASHIONNA
CONSTRUCTION DIRECTION: ISHIMARU COMPANY

WITH THANKS TO I.T. COMPANY FOR THEIR BELIEF AND ENTHUSIASM AND WITH WHOM IT HAS BEEN A PLEASURE TO WORK ON THIS SHOP.

20 ON LAN STREET, CENTRAL, HONG KONG

COMME des GARÇONS
20 ON LAN STREET, CENTRAL, HONG KONG

*Jimi*Hendrix

For Alain Dister's photographic exhibition "Riding in the Wind, the Jimi Hendrix Years" at Agnès b. Librairie Galerie, the gallery produced a necklace strung onto a guitar with four colored picks bearing a message about the artist and rock'n'roll music, written by Agnès b. herself.

cl.   Agnès b. Librairie Galerie
y.   2006
CC   *exhibition*

*Two*Faced

The exhibition "Two Faced – The Changing Face of Portraiture" showcased portraits by paired image-makers in a happening to produce each other's portraits. In addition, the show exhibited a selection of contemporary portraits of influencial individuals in the creative industries in the 21st century, and reinterpreted them from a new angle. The souvenir gift of the exhibition opening, featuring an interactive performance by Spring Poetry Dance Group, was a flat hand-mirror, allowing guests to reflect upon themselves.

cl.   Agnès b. Librairie Galerie, WIWP, IdN
y.   2007
CC   *exhibition*

Suitman **Forever**

Artist Young Kim, a.k.a. Suitman, has traveled around the world with his suit and camera, leaving only a footprint behind. For his "Suitman: Forever" show held in three Agnès b. stores in Taiwan, he enlarged his Suitman photos into giant prints for the grand atrium. Exhibition souvenirs included gold and silver Suitman figurines, Suitman medals and camera tote bags.

cl.   *Agnès b. Librairie Galerie*
y.   *2006*

CC   *exhibition*

SuitmanHK Invasion

When Suitman invaded Hong Kong, he meant business in the territory. People posed for their portraits wearing the infamous suit on the street, which were then exhibited alongside Young Kim's own 14-year travel photos from around the world. At the exhibition's grand opening, breakdancers hid inside 6-foot inflatable Suitman figures to bring them suddenly to life on the basement gallery floor. Each guest received their very own 2-foot inflatable Suitman figure to bring home.

cl.   *Agnès b. Librairie Galerie*
y.   *2005*
CC *exhibition*

*HelloKitty*SecretHouse

As one of the world's most recognizable icons of cute, Hello Kitty hides many secrets. The "Hello Kitty Secret House" exhibition invited visitors to embark on a journey through her world of interactive installations and retrospective exhibitions, between familiar images, artistic interpretations and the public's own imagination.

cd.   *AllRightsReserved Ltd.*
cl.   *AllRightsReserved Ltd., Sanrio*
y.   *2006*

 exhibition

TDTDE Exhibition

The "Total Design" exhibition, held in Cibone's Aoyama shop in 2004, showcased the work of influential design groups from Amsterdam and the rest of the world. Promotional material successfully underlined the importance of brand identity. More novelty items included a poster (cover) and a retrospective picture book featuring designs for clients such as KLM, Heineken and Esquire.

d.   CIBONE
y.   2004
🅒🅒   *exhibition*

Cibone Plane

This model airplane was the novelty item of Cibone's lifestyle-editorial shop opening – a symbol of their take-off into the world as a new brand from Tokyo in 2001. Decorated with Cibone's logotype and corporate colors, the miniature jet was distributed to guests during the reception, along with original coasters featuring items in the shop.

d.   CIBONE
y.   2001
🔅   *new shop/company*

Willy Wonka **TV Room Goggle**

Special thanks to Warner Bros. Entertainment Inc

"It's television not telephone, it's quite different." said Willy Wonka, which is particularly true for Wonka's invention, allowing people in and out, which is not available in real world. The goggle can delight die-hard fans and lovers of crazy novelty gifts alike. Each shiny pinkish lens measures a whopping 3-inches in diameter while the Wonka logo graces either side. Although the glasses look crazy from the outside, the wearer can see just fine when wearing these spectacular spectacles. These white plastic glasses have a high quality stretchable and adjustable strap and are one size fits all – and suitable for those who cannot think and only sees too!

f.   *Warner Bros Pictures Int'l*
y.   *2005*
     movie

*Bigger*Returns

Arc Worldwide Malaysia organized a retail-marketing seminar to teach marketers how to use Arc's proprietary tools to future-proof their brands. All seminar attendees received a personalized thank-you pack as an invitation to maximize their return on investment from the seminar. Delivered in the form of a giant wallet, Arc pitched the opportunity to gain bigger market share with a mega-sized, customized bank note that let clients sample their ArcAudit tool (worth USD10,000) for a special fee of only RM100. To introduce an additional sense of urgency, the trial offer was limited to a three-day period.

cd.   Tan Kien Eng
ad.   Theresa Tsang/Tan Kien Eng
d.   Theresa Tsang
c.   Valerie Chen
ph.   Allen Dang, Wizard Photography
i.   Khairul Anuar
f.   Arc Worldwide
cl.   Arc Worldwide
y.   2006

  advertising

  branding

Switching To **Off Lo Hi**

Off-lo-hi is a production workshop based in Hong Kong, founded by directors David Pun and Alfred Hau. Inspired by the knobs of air-conditioning controls in cars, the three words "off", "low" and "high" represent their creative flexibility, from silently elegant to shockingly climactic. Translating this philosophy into a sensory design, Off-lo-hi's introduction gift was a tiny box with a shaker connected to the adjuster, so that people could feel varying levels of vibration, as if testing the pulse of the company with a tangible tremor.

ad.   David Pun (Off-lo-hi Ltd.),
       Godfrey Kwan (Junkie Design)
d.   Godfrey (Junkie Design)
cl.   Off-lo-hi Ltd.
y.   2002

new shop/company

*PingPong*Action

As the post-production house Ping Pong believes that creativity is driven by interaction
between elements, their opening party favor
was a tube of table-tennis balls – to encourage
people to interact with each other.

ad. *David Pun (Off-lo-hi Ltd.)*
d.   *David Pun (Off-lo-hi Ltd.)*
i.   *Godfrey (Junkie Design)*
cl. *PING PONG*
y.   *2003*

 new shop/company

*WataruKomachi*Show

The opening exhibition of Cibone's gallery space spotlighted distinctive works by artist Wataru Komachi, whose themes are "Melody Fair" (gentle, clean, transparent) and "Silky" (urban elegance). Komachi's collage poster was given to guests of the opening reception.

d.   Wataru Komachi
y.   2006
ⓒⓒ *exhibition*

Chocolate&Cake

Observing the "White Christmas" tradition, this holiday cream cake is actually a leather pouch, with a strawberry brooch and candy key ring. As the Christmas spirit is translated into an everyday practical item, shoppers can redeem their purchases for the leather cake, while profits are donated to the cancer fund.

ad.   AllRightsReserved Ltd.
at.   Tadaaki Wakamatsu (Q-pot)
cl.   Harbour City
y.   2006

advertising

100%ChocolateCafe.

100% Chocolate Cafe. selected 365 different flavors of chocolate for each day of the year to form an edible gourmet calendar. Any customer who has a drink in the cafe can also receive one free chocolate day, while 20-day chocolate packs are also available for purchase in the shop. The 365-day idea was extremely popular, as special holidays, such as Valentine's Day and Christmas, sold out in 30 minutes.

d.   groovisions
y.   since 2005
cl. MEIJI SEIKA KAISHA, LTD

branding   product launch

*365Days***Chocolates**

マクダル
パイナップル
パン王子

McDull,
Prince de
la Bun

www.mc

MARCH

ユーロスペース
EUROSPACE
T. 03.3461.0211

ブタニダッテテカコハアル

McDull, PrinceDeLaBun

McDull/Movie

As the second McDull animated feature film, "McDull, Prince de la Bun" reprised its textured stories of Hong Kong past and present in contrasting graphics. To capture the attention of the Japanese audience, the designers pulled out the bright pink and yellow visuals of the little cartoon pig and his pineapple bun for all localized main visuals and premiums. Die-cut leaflets, flyers, tote bags, coasters and badges were distributed during the holidays in Shibuya, on one of Tokyo's busiest, trendiest street corners.

ad. groovisions
d.   groovisions
cl. magic hour
y.   2006
✺   *movie*

*HarmonicaBldg*LittleBlackRidingHood

The children's story of "Little Red Riding Hood" (Aka-zukin Chan), inspired these illustrations and stuffed toy, in which the girl wears a black cloak and the wolf is replaced by a dog to celebrate the Year of the Dog in a lunar new year gift. The stuffed dog is filled with toy balls, while the illustrations tell the story of the black dog and "Little Black Riding Hood".

f.   *harmonica bldg.*
y.   *2006*
 branding

102

*DanceArtist*Auditions!

France's contemporary dance center and theater commissioned a call for auditions using free-flowing pink elves that jump out of the bag to greet and invite young people to join overseas dance-education exchange programs. Stickers and postcards were distributed to the public during the promotion.

ad.   Antoine + Manuel
cl.   *Centre National de Danse Contemporaine*
y.   *2006*

advertising

*Hiroshima***Renewal**

A branded box of Kintaro candy was offered as the opening gift to guests joining the celebration of the renewed BEAMS BOY shop in Hiroshima. Traditionally, Kintaro candies bless children so that they grow up to be strong and happy. This colorful twist on an age-old custom invited shop customers to share the sweet joy of BEAMS' rebirth.

d.   *BEAMS creative*
y.   *2003*

✂ *shop opening*

*BEAMS'***30thAnniv.**

Celebrating BEAMS' 30-year retrospective of success in the fashion industry, this audio CD documents the all the soundbites that ritually go into aiming to please every customer. Featuring interviews with contributing creators and planners of the commemorative event, this CD souvenir was offered to guests at BEAMS' 30th-anniversary celebration dinner in Tokyo in 2006.

d.   *BEAMS creative*
y.   *2006*

◈ *anniversary*

Bags With Satisfaction

As shopping at BEAMS always brings about a bagful of satisfaction, specially crafted shopping bags are designed for different occasions, from a new-shop launch party to a veteran-shop anniversary celebration.

Blue nylon bag, Bandana, Orange tote bag, Creamy cotton bag

d.   *BEAMS creative*
y.   *2006*

✂ *shop opening*   ▦ *advertising*

*BEAMSBOY*Kit

As the BEAMS BOY line is BEAMS for girls, BEAMS made a souvenir sewing kit just for the gals, with an important message: Be cool like the boys. The traditionally girly kit - comprising needle, thread, scissors, pins and buttons on heart-shaped cardboard - is packaged in a boyishly hard, round, metal can. Most importantly, it contains the novelty BEAMS BOY patch, which can be used to brand any stray garment in the mending pile.

d. *BEAMS creative*
y. *2006*

◇ *anniversary*

*Monogram*Bags

As Mexican Mania was the theme for BEAMS BOY summer fashion series in 2004-2005, the Mexican summer energy was translated into colorful prints of flowers, fruits and guitars. These patterns were then blended with BEAMS BOY monograms and manufactured into branded shopping bags.

d. *BEAMS creative*
y. *2004-2005*

✳ *advertising*

Tachikawa**Opening**

For all those who just can't wait, this shop-opening invitation card provides a checklist for previewing all the fashionable goods that will fit in your closet. The invitation also includes a floating-logo ball-point pen, so that you can jot down your wishlist ahead of the launch.

d.   *BEAMS creative*
y.   *2005, 2006*

♦   *anniversary*
✂   *shop opening*

RenewalParty**Invitation**

Around 2004, BEAMS decided to extend its collections from hip-hop streetwear to sophisticated suits by establishing various theme shops in Harajuku, Tokyo. To inaugurate the first volume of the Harajuku street project, the opening-party invitation to BEAMS' renewed shop popped up to present an open door into the brand-new shopping environment.

d.   *BEAMS creative*
y.   *2004*

♦   *anniversary*
✂   *shop opening*

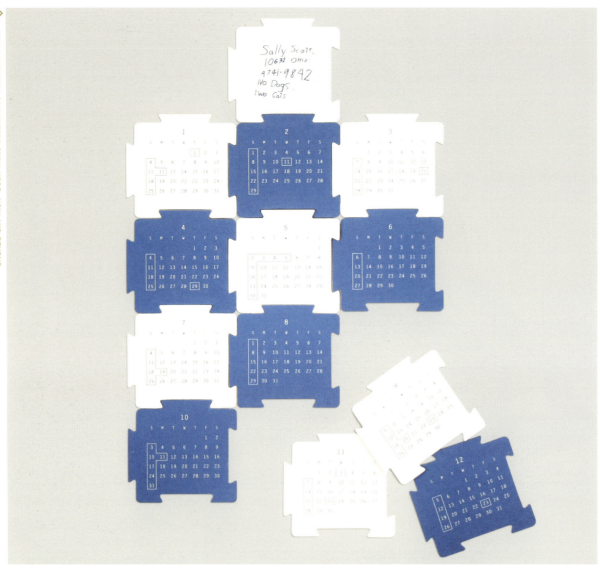

*SallyScott*PuzzleCalendar

This 12-month calendar made up of blue and white puzzle pieces was the novelty item of Sally Scott's "Make a Christmas!" winter fair. The campaign proposed various styles of merry Christmas-themed one-piece dresses. The puzzle calendar was the prize souvenir awarded to the first 30 customers to make a purchase at the shop during the campaign.

ad. Atsuki Kikuchi
d.   Atsuki Kikuchi (Bluemark)
cl. Sally Scott
y.   2004

 branding 🌼 advertising

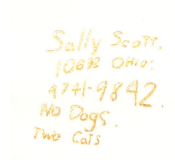

Sally Scott **5thAnniversaryDM/Note**

This original notebook and DM were created especially to commemorate fashion brand Sally Scott's 5th anniversary. The notebook features 20 posters displayed at Sally Scott shops over the past five years to illustrate the history of the brand. The novelties were given out as party favors to all purchasing customers at the shop during the anniversary campaign.

ad.   Atsuki Kikuchi
d.   Atsuki Kikuchi (Bluemark)
cl.   Sally Scott
y.   2007

◇   anniversary

JAGDA Picture Pencil

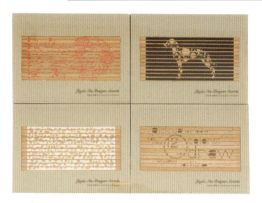

Four winners of the JAGDA New Designer Awards 2005 volunteered to create this colored-pencil set for their commemorative exhibition in 2005-2006. The foursome also inspired the numerical theme, manifest in the pencils' quadrilateral cross-section and four different "puzzle" patterns.

cl. *Team JAGDA New Designer Awards 2005*
ad. *Takahisa Nakajima*
cd. *Takahisa Nakajima, Koji Iyama,*
     Chiharu Kondo, Kazushi "sabi" Nakanishi
d.   *Takahisa Nakajima, Koji Iyama,*
     Chiharu Kondo, Kazushi "sabi" Nakanishi
y.   *2005*

CC *exhibition*

Bally **Pencils**

As the shoe factory renowned for its antique fine leather products, Bally manufactured as a complimentary gift this mini pencil set. The finely stitched leather case carries the hallmark of a hot-stamp embossed brand logo on dark bronze crocodile leather.

f.   *Bally*

♛ *branding*

*NodameCantabile***OriginalDiary**

This novelty agenda, themed after the TV drama series "Nodame Cantabile", was offered to magazine readers and website viewers of the show. Based on the story of piano student Nodame and her friends at a music college, the diary uses the piano keyboard for the cover design, while inside pages are printed in beige to imitate the retro visual style of student music notebooks.

ad. *Chizuru Suematsu*
d.   *Hiroyasu Ito*
y.   *2006*

✹ *advertising*

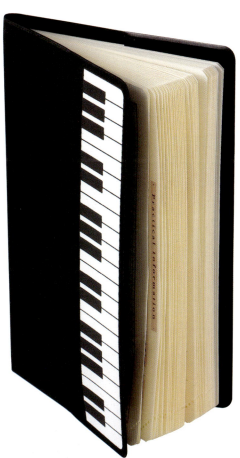

*Canon*MiniatureCamera

Celebrating the launch of Canon's newest digital camera, Canon collaborated with Winson Creation to make this limited-edition miniature model in a ratio of 1:6. All parts and camera components can be assembled to function just like the real thing.

f.   Canon

👑 *branding* ★ *by collectors*

PHaTPHOTO35mmPinholeCamera

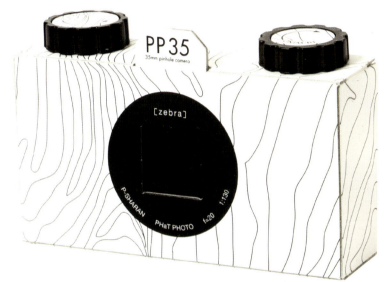

This DIY paper pinhole camera was distributed as a supplement to the photo magazine "PHaT PHOTO" Vol.27 in May-June, 2005. As opposed to the traditionally black body of most cameras for light blocking, this novelty gadget was designed in white, so that people could customize their own camera by painting or pasting on various wallpapers. Another highlighted feature is the camera's exceptionally light paper body, designed in the smallest size for using 35mm film. Extra of 2nd edition "tigre" is the square photo-framing, as an advance of its former edition "zebra".

cl.   CMS Corp., "PHaT PHOTO"
ad. Atsushi Takeda (SOUVENIR DESIGN)
d.   Atsushi Takeda (SOUVENIR DESIGN)
y.   April 2005

advertising

To promote the hit movie based on the bitter-sweet TV drama, souvenir T-shirts and caps parody its themes. The five main characters are designed around the central themes of baseball and death, as the main players of a high-school baseball team. The commemorative book set includes a towel and a pen in the shape of a wooden bat.

Shinushinu-dan (dead boys) T-shirt/Cap
d.   BEAMS
cl.   Round
y.   2006

Official Memorial Box
p.   Magazine House
y.   2006

❌   *movie*

© KCEWS2006

*KisarazuCat'sEye**WorldSeries**

*Ecole*Movie

As the movie "Ecole" is set in a girls' school, its promotional visuals drew on that very particular environment. Reflecting the various facets of the young girls' personalities on stationery and polaroids, all promotional material was conscientiously designed to ripple the visual, tactile and sixth senses of the audience, recalling the film's mysterious atmosphere.

ad.   *Mari Iwanami (xenon)*
y.   *2006*
✖   *movie*

Crow & Trash

The award-winning card game *Crow & Trash* uses 12 cards printed on both sides, where the object of the game is to turn over all the cards to the player's chosen side. The designer deck was presented as a souvenir item at the National Modern Art Museum in Tokyo.

ad. WABISABI (Ryohey "wabi" Kudo, Kazushi "sabi" Nakanishi)
ph. Mikio Ishizaki (crow), Ryohey "wabi" Kudo (trash)
y. 2004

▷ *product launch*
▪ *new shop/company*

*WabiSabi*Hormones

"Hormones" is a typography set created by Sapporo design group WABISABI. Inspired by the dynamic protean combination of hormone cells, the various patterns were developed with embedded text and messages. The signature design is applied to WABISABI's company gifts, to be distributed as stylish souvenirs.

ad. WABISABI (Ryohey "wabi" Kudo, Kazushi "sabi" Nakanishi)

♛ *branding*

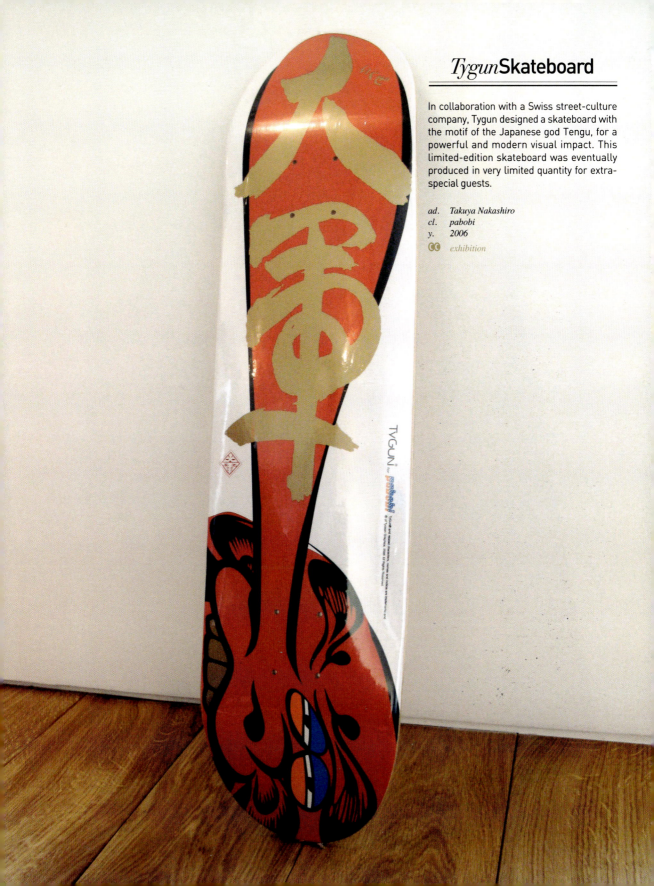

*Tygun*Skateboard

In collaboration with a Swiss street-culture company, Tygun designed a skateboard with the motif of the Japanese god Tengu, for a powerful and modern visual impact. This limited-edition skateboard was eventually produced in very limited quantity for extra-special guests.

ad.   *Takuya Nakashiro*
cl.   *pabobi*
y.   *2006*
CC *exhibition*

御祝

*Uniqlo*FuroshikiGift

Cashmere is usually an expensive item in the fashion industry, but Uniqlo has given it an affordable package. Based on the concept "traditional and pop", the cashmere muffler is presented inside a gift box made from paulownia wood and special wrapping cloth, thus emphasizing the bargain around the elegance.

cd.   Kashiwa Sato
ad.   Kashiwa Sato
d.   Ko Ishikawa
y.   2006

♛ branding

OPENING OF

GLOBAL FLAGSHIP

NEW YORK

EMBER 9TH 2006 / 8-10 P.M.

BETWEEN PRINCE AND SPRING

.com

TO NEW YORK

FROM TOKYO TO NEW YO

CELEBRATE THE OPENING

THE UNIQLO SO

GLOBAL FLAGSH

UNI QLO

TO NEW YORK

From Tokyo To New York

From its original cradle in Tokyo to its new flagship shop in New York City, Uniqlo invites the community from the West to experience the wind from the East. The "Sense invitation" was delivered in the form of a handy paper fan, stamped with its brand logo printed in both English and Japanese katakana characters, fusing pop and exotic impressions.

cd.   Kashiwa Sato
ad.   Kashiwa Sato
d.   Ko Ishikawa
y.   2006

 new shop/company
branding

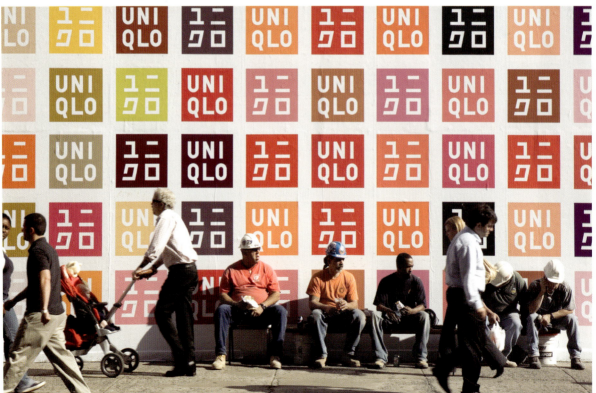

*FromTokyo*ToNewYork

Presenting their new flagship store as both strongly branded and adapted especially to New Yorkers, Uniqlo introduced themselves with the free magazine "Uniqlo Paper", featuring up-to-date news, tee-art and coupons. Also seen around the city were 13 different artwork shopping bags and various urban media branded with their signature red and white square.

Shopping bags
cd. Kashiwa Sato
ad. Kashiwa Sato
d.   Ko Ishikawa

Uniqlo Paper
cd. Markus Kiersztan (MP Creative)
ad. Markus Kiersztan (MP Creative)
y.   2006

new shop/company   branding

*Uniqlo*TeeExhibition

Uniqlo believes T-shirts are walking art galleries that deliver the messages of the people wearing them. So the souvenir packaging for Uniqlo's T-shirt (UT.) exhibition is designed like a postal-delivery service envelope. Inside was a plain black T-shirt and a stencil message board, so that guests could spray-paint their own tee.

ad.   *Tripster*
d.   *7STARS DESIGN*
y.   *2007*
CC   *exhibition*

*UniqloTeeExhibition*UT.PhilosophyBehindT-shirt

*FinePaper*Premiums

While metallic paper may seem too fancy for everyday items, Takeo Fine Paper decided to make fine-paper premiums for its 2007 paper show in Tokyo. Anyone shopping in the vicinity of the Ginza gallery during the exhibition period could receive the fine-paper goods, from playing cards to a mini tissue box, by making purchases in the 26 shops from the A-to-Z fine-paper premium network.

cl.   *Takeo Fine Paper*
y.   *2007*
        exhibition

ALLINONE

Banking service should be advanced to centralize all complicated steps in one. With this idea, THE NISHI-NIPPON CITY BANK and creative unit groovisions developed a black dog character. Upon its unique but high plasticity form, various premium novelty goods are produced and deliverd to customers to let them familiarize the character natually in daily life at home or at the office. Combining high usability and clean designs, ALLINONE becomes an iconic image that projecting the bank's prompt and superior service.

ad.   groovisions, Takao Ito
d.   Tadashi Cho, Taisuke Matsuoka,
      Tsubasa Takasu
ch.   groovisions
pl.   Takao Ito, Kenichiro Yamamoto,
      Tadashi Cho
cl.   THE NISHI-NIPPON CITY BANK, LTD.
y.   2005-2007
♛   branding

THE NISHI-NIPPON CITY BANK

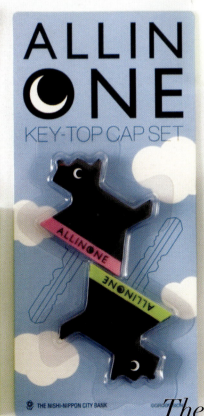

TheNishi-NipponCity Bank

*GroundZero*HardestDreamtoDream

The "Hardest Dream to Dream" theme of Ground Zero's S/S 06 collection was meant to reflect what is inside people's minds around the world today: fear, insecurity, uncertainty, hope, desire. Unique graphics used as metaphors for these irrational emotions became the eclectic pattern for this socially aware fashion series. Souvenir items offered a closer glimpse of each designer's inspirations through View-master slides.

f.   Ground Zero
y.   2006
fashion show

*GroundZero***CloseLookToBackground**

*Nike*LaserProject

On the road to innovation, creative design on sneakers goes well beyond mere stitches and patches. Using laser engraving on the sneaker not only introduced contrasting textures, it offered fine-gradation details and graphics on the same material through 3D laser cutting. The souvenir of the laser project exhibition was a leather card holder with a complex laser-engraved pattern as a beautiful example of this advanced technique.

f.   *Nike*
y.   *2006*
      product launch
      exhibition

*Mastermind*10thAnniversary

Street fashion brand mastermind is stepping into their 10th anniversary, this die-cut invitation card was designed with the brands iconic identity, the skull. The logo and the frame were embossed with vintage patterns on pearly silver hard cards.

f.   *mastermind*
y.   *2007*
      anniversary

*FORETAUTUMN*NoveltyHandkerchief

This dainty yellow handkerchief was designed according to the "autumn" theme of FORET's seasonal 2005 collection. The finest material was selected to make the highest-quality handkerchief, while the silhouette of forest trees, as the key visual of the campaign, was illustrated on the sheer fabric underneath a white square decorated with a classic cross-pattern of icons.

ad.   *Shinsuke Koshio/SUNDAY VISION*
cl.   *Laforet HARAJUKU*
y.   *2005*

advertising

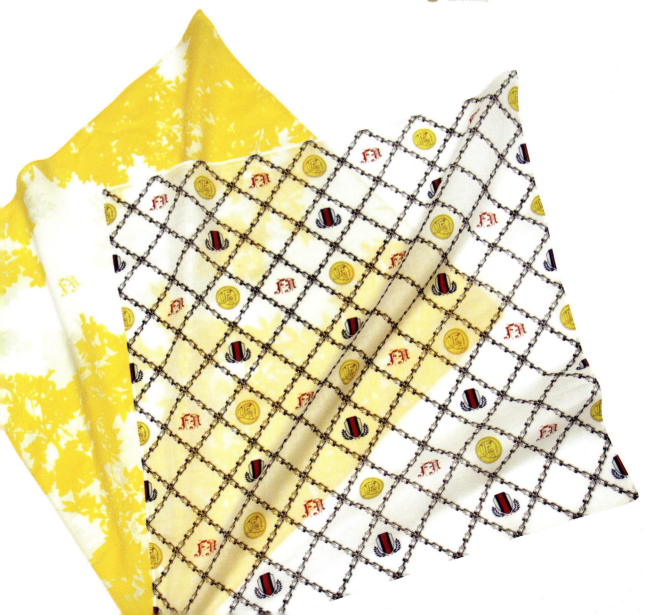

6.5Billions'Survival/**Exhibition**

6.5Billions' Survival

The walk-through interactive exhibition 6.5 billions' Survival – Living, with Emerging Sciences explores the frontiers of science in terms of human survival under the five themes of energy, food, living environment, tools and communication. Using the life jacket as a motif, the environmental design presents both the benefits and harms of technology, inviting visitors to reconsider the facts from the data provided in the survival-kit booklet.

ad. Masahito Hanzawa, Junya Saito
d.   Masahito Hanzawa, Junya Saito
f.   Power Graphixx Inc.
cl. National Museum of Emerging Science
     and Innovation (Miraikan)
y.   2006

 exhibition

Kami-Robo LiveEventPromotion

Kami-Robo Live

Kami-Robo are robots made of paper, all 15 to 20 centimeters tall. Each one has its own name and personality, while friendships and alliances form and break during their fights. In 2006, the live event "Maoh vs Blue Killer" presented a mixture of pro wrestling, film, theater and Kami-Robo fighting in Tokyo's Omotesando Hills, with souvenir free paper and DVD. At the robot expo held at London's ICA, over one hundred original Kami-Robo models, iconography and other paraphernalia were exhibited, with a vacuum-sealed sticker and postcard series as premiums. In 2005, visitors of the Ginza Graphic Gallery received mini plastic "Kami-Keshi" figurines from the vending machine, along with novelty Kami-Robo beer sold over the counter.

ad. Katsunori Aoki
ch. Tomohiro Yasui
i. Tamio Abe
p. Takakazu Aoyama, Tomohiro Yasui,
     Ooda Eiji
f. butterfly-stroke inc.
cl. butterfly-stroke inc.
y. 2005, 2006

 exhibition *branding*

*Fahrenheit*911

Promotional posters of the movie "Fahrenheit 9/11" were designed in the form of paper face masks bearing the image of either the film's director Michael Moore or U.S. President George W. Bush. The face masks were distributed to the audience at preview screenings, where guests were free to express their support for either side, depending on which mask they chose to wear.

ad. *Katsunori Aoki*
d.   *Kana Takakuwa, Fumio Tachibana*
i.   *Bunpei Yorifuji*
f.   *butterfly-stroke inc.*
cl. *GAGA COMMUNICATIONS INC.*
y.   *2004*

✖ *movie*

Design Tide is an annual event presenting
design-related seminars and exhibitions in
Tokyo. In 2005 and 2006, special ties were created for the festival: thick cotton-wool green
ties to give participating artists a playful
casual look at the closing party; white and
black "blank & peace" ties printed with the Design Tide watermark in 2006, worn by staff and
available for purchase by festival attendees.

ad.   *Masamichi Toyama*
d.   *Yuko Nakamura*
cl.   *giraffe*
y.   *2006*
▶   *product launch*
CC   *exhibition*

*GiraffeDesignTideTie&NewTies***LaunchParty**

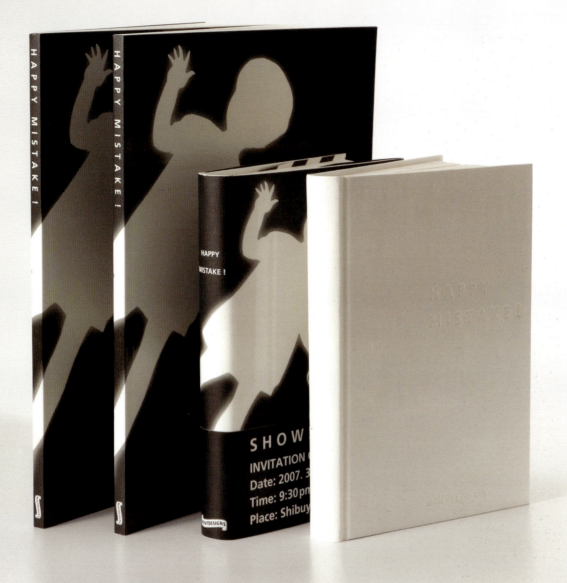

mintdesignsFW0708

Tying in the two themes of bookshop and sleep, mint designs' F/W 0708 show "Midnight Book Club" took place in a real book store. After business hours, all shelves were filled with the "Happy Mistake!" books specially designed for the show. Guests could use their book-cover invitation to wrap up the evening's novelty gift – the midnight-book-club book, making a special appearance on the catwalk as hair accessory and prop.

ad.   mint designs
d.   mint designs
ph.   Yoshitsugu Enomoto
y.   2007

 fashion show

*mintdesigns***FW0708**

Real/PaperButtons

Ever since its establishment in 2001, mint designs has issued a series of novelty paper buttonsheets. The buttons, each featuring the theme color or fabric of each collection, are made of vulcanized fiber and can be removed and sewn onto actual clothing. The Mondrian series, inspired by the Dutch painter Piet Mondrian, was produced in association with the live silk-screening fashion show.

d. mint designs
y. 2001-2005

fashion show   branding

mintdesigns **MondrianSeries**

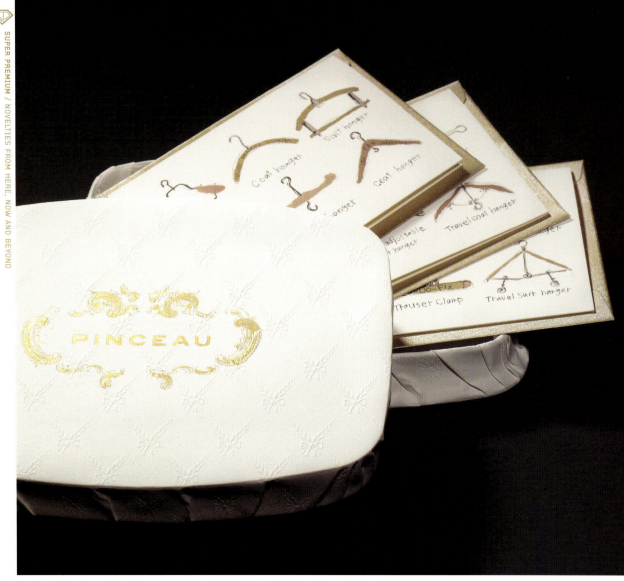

*Pinceau*GiftBox

Fashion brand Pinceau aims to assist each individual to paint their own colors on the canvas of their life, offering particle ladies' clothing with "good old style". This delicately embossed gift box contains four sets of greeting cards and envelopes, with casual illustrations introducing various types of hangers.

ad. *Naomi Hirabayashi*
d. *Natsuko Yoneyama*
i. *Kiyomi Nakagawa*
cl. *Takeo Co., Ltd.*
y. *2007*
ⓒⓒ *exhibition*

MarieAntoinette

To commemorate her friend Sofia Coppola's movie "Marie Antoinette", loosely based on the historical biography *Marie Antoinette: The Journey*, Anna Sui created a special cosmetics gift box available exclusively in Japan. Containing a precious powder puff and lavishly decorated with silks, sweets and roses, the limited-edition premium was sold out soon after its movie-screening launch.

d.   Anna Sui
y.   2007
✕ *movie*

Marie Antoinette
マリー・アントワネット

coccaFlagshipStoreOpening

Textile brand cocca specializes in original cloth, patterns and textile design. The invitation to the grand opening of its flagship store was printed on uniquely patterned cloth with dyed details, while its business cards double as thread coils to reflect the brand's handmade, tactile identity. cocca extended its exquisite design to its souvenir button-shaped cookies and a pocket tissue case, handy novelties to nibble on and sniffle into every day.

Opening invitation/shop DM
d.   *KLOKA GRAPHICS*
cl.   *cocca*

Pocket tissue cover
d.   *spoken words project*
cl.   *cocca*

Button cookies
ad. *Baden Baden*
d.   *milkey pop*
cl.   *cocca*
y.   *2006*

 new shop/company

*CrystalBall/*2007Premiums

Premiums represent history in an anthropological sense, and you can track events and celebrations through them. In the first half of 2007, Crystal Ball came up with a spate of gifts, including various stickers like Hippie Photo, Groovin'High Mirror, Merci, Groovin' High Collage, Crystal Ball Wall, Jeremy Scott Collaboration, Love Hippie & Beach Mirror and Hippie & Beach Photo. Besides, there are 8th Anniversary Key Chains and Crystal Ball / GARCIA MARQUEZ gauche Premium Book vol. 2 Bags & Scarves, which are gifts with the right purchase at the right time.

f.   HDR, Inc. / Crystal Ball
y.   2007

  branding

Donald/Diesel

Diesel and Amsterdam agency Kesselskramer took a swipe at emotion-based branding in S/S 02 by envisaging a park called Happy Valley, in which consumers' cares disappeared. The world was overseen by the disturbing Donald Diesel, boosting Diesel's reputation as a brand that credits its consumers with some intelligence. Happy customers could bring home a souvenir Donald figurine and cup.

cd.   *Diesel Creative Team, Kesselskramer*
y.   *2002*

advertising

i-D *Diesel***AtCentralHongKong**

To honor the longstanding relationship between Diesel and i-D magazine, the two fashion-lifestyle brands collaborated on "The White Trash Issue" in Hong Kong. Black and white editions of i-D×Diesel tote bags contained The White Trash Issue and the i-D Safe & Sound book. i-D magazine's creative team also designed a special window display of Asian faces from The White Trash Issue for the Diesel store in Central, Hong Kong.

d.   *i-D × Diesel Creative Team*
y.   *2007*
♛ *branding*

DenimCampaign **SS07**

Diesel traditionally gives its different styles of its denim unique and quirky names. For its S/S 07 denim campaign, Diesel made use of these names in tongue-in-cheek phrases plastered across billboards throughout the campaign. The key slogan was "I would look good on you", which was printed in big black letters on the wooden cover of the catalogue, postcard book, badges and paper bags.

d.   *Diesel Creative Team*
y.   *2007*

🌼   *advertising*

*DenimCampaign*SS03

"Keep Fit, Stop Dieting, Stick to Diesel" was the message for Diesel's daring denim campaign for S/S 03. The message was that Diesel denim can make you look good, no matter what your body shape. The S/S 03 denim promotional box even included a real chocolate bar and "stop dieting" chocolate mirror, reminding each customer that no matter what they eat, they'll always look good in Diesel jeans.

d.   *Diesel Creative Team*
y.   *2003*

✹   *advertising*

Diesel Yamme Lappi-Latino

Lappi-Latino was one of the key motifs for Diesel's F/W 04 collection, where the Lappi Latino cartoon character was a key graphic for the season. The campaign souvenir gift was a bright orange portable cushion that customers could use as fashionably as they pleased.

d.   *Diesel Creative Team*
y.   *2004*

advertising

OH-OKU Tea

Japanese tea gifts packaged in traditionally round containers were created as novelty items for the TV drama series "OH-OKU", which told stories of Japan's inner palace in the 17th-19th centuries. Flamboyant multicolored patterns of Japanese picture scrolls were mapped onto the cans, and later reappeared as motifs on the posters.

cd.   *Taeko Ohtsubo*
ad.   *Eiji Yamada*
d.   *Chiharu Kondo*
i.   *Keiichiro Ohshima*
y.   *2005*

advertising

Agnèsb. FreeCondoms

Well-known for her humanitarian actions and social awareness, Agnès b. distributes free condoms in her stores and has been committed to the battle against AIDS from the beginning. In 2005, Agnès b. donated 20,000 condoms to be distributed in Swaziland and South Africa. Each year, over 1.5 million condoms are handed out in France, with slogans written by Agnès herself.

f.   *Agnès b.*
♛   *branding*

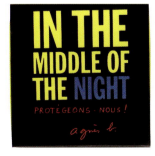

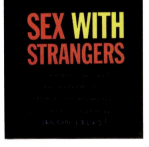

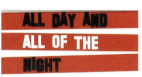

*KubrickNikeDesign-*Generation2

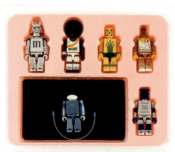

Generation 2 was the second memorable collaboration between Medicom Toy and Nike, after the huge success of Kubrick Nike Design-Generation 1. The special collection, limited to 1,500 sets worldwide, included six 60mm midgets: "Funk Soul" by Sean Barret; "AfterShox" by Steve Phemister; "Brasil" by Greg Hoffman; "Liquid Sport" by Andy Walker; "Fugu" by Lance Lovett; "Double Dutch" by Richard Clark & Nicole Mueller. Also enclosed was a booklet offering an exclusive peek inside the eccentric minds of six Nike designers.

f.   *Medicom Toy, Nike*
y.   *2004*

    advertising

*TestPatrol/*FW05

Following Diesel's F/W 05 "Wild Wild East" theme, a special charms key chain was produced as a souvenir for Diesel's seasonal staff training program. All participants received a charms key chain with cactus, police patches, cowboys, dice and key with pointer light.

d.   *Diesel Creative Team*
y.   *2005*
♔   *branding*

*TestPatrol/*SS07

As the theme of the S/S 07 collection was "air", the look and feel of the seasonal training program (Test Patrol) was inspired by an airport lobby, where even the training schedule was printed on a flight-timetable template. The premium was a travel kit normally distributed during long-haul flights.

d.   *Diesel Creative Team*
y.   *2007*
♔   *branding*

©KAWS,, 06

Original Fake ShopOpening

*OriginalFake*ShopOpening

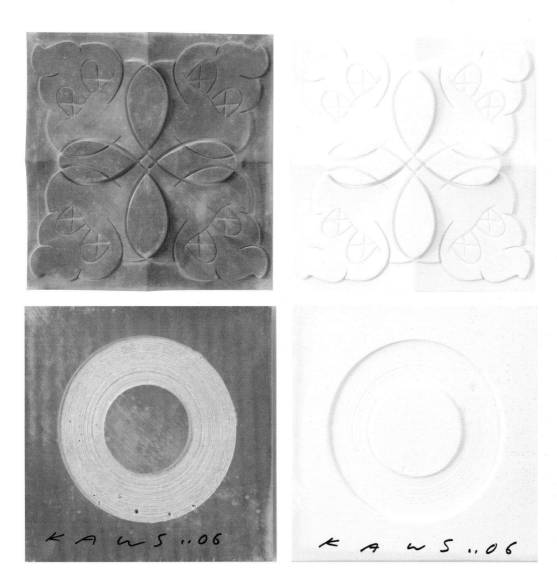

*OriginalFake*ShopOpening

A collaborative campaign between KAWS and MEDICOM TOY, this concept store played not only on the words "original" and "fake" but also on the theme of "co-habitation of contrary elements". The giant figurine stood in the middle of the store as a provocative dividing element, custom designed by KAWS. The shop interior is divided into half from the central vertical axis of the figure, while the tiles are shaded in white and gray tones. The opening-party souvenir gifts were real tiles from the shop signed by KAWS.

f.   *OriginalFake*
in. *Masamichi Katayama (Wonderwall Inc.)*
y.   *2006*

 new shop/company

*PlayColorful*Akibaman

As the theme of the Nike iD campaign was Play Colorful, brightly colored characters were used to catch people's eyes. Dressed from head to toe in a colorful cosplay jumpsuit and matching Nike shoes, Akibaman chases dully clad businessmen in black and gray suits. The mini Akibaman figures were distributed as novelty souvenirs of the Nike iD shoe's customized service, so customers could individually design the playful avatar's shoes, clothing and accessories to match their own style – or improve their performance.

f.   Nike
y.   2006

*1Love*NikeAF1×Hectic

The 1LOVE store is a one-year concept shop celebrating the 25th anniversary of AF1. Customers who buy AF1 at 1LOVE are eligible for a lucky lottery draw, while winners are awarded free premium laser etching on their newly purchased pair of Nikes, with a choice of white, black or bare laser etching.

cl.   Nike Japan
y.   2007

   advertising,

25 YEARS OF UNDISPUTED LOVE
NIGHT OF CELEBRATION
JANUARY 6, 2007, 9:00 PM
CENTRAL STAR FERRY PIER NO.7
GENTLEMEN MUST WEAR SNEAKERS
INVITE ONLY, NON-TRANSFERABLE

RSVP
MARIA LEUNG
MARIA@ARANVIBE.COM
852 3106 0492

SINCE 1982, AIR FORCE 1 IS A
LANDMARK OF FINE HERITAGE IN
SPORT, CULTURE AND BEYOND
LIKEWISE, THE DELICATE WAX SEAL
HAS LONG BEEN THE CLASSIC
HALLMARK OF FINESSE. THIS PREMIUM
BOX SET IS BOTH AN EXCLUSIVE TOKEN
OF AF1'S CRAFTSMANSHIP AND AN
EXCEPTIONAL SOUVENIR OF THIS
HISTORICAL "1 NIGHT".

Celebrating 25 years since Nike Air Force 1 launched its first shoes in 1982, the AF1 anniversary party paid tribute to its origins – music, breakdance, street culture – with an exhibition of interactive installations, motion graphics, and a showcase of AF1's unique history. This same occasion saw the launch of Nike's latest AF1 design at Central Star Ferry Pier No.7 in Hong Kong in January 2007. The invitation card reprised the star-patterns of AF1's signature sole, embossed on tactile white paper and sealed with gold wax. The Nike Air Force 1 branded stamp announced a hallmark of fine quality to set the tone for the evening ahead.

ad.   *AllRightsReserved Ltd.*
cl.   *Nike*
y.   *2007*

◇   *anniversary*

*SealingStamps*AirForceTurns25HK

*Chocolate*AirForce1

In celebration of Air Force 1's 25th anniversary, +41 produced Mini Choco Sneakers: Air Force 1 White Chocolate and Dunks:Trainers:Blazers Dark Chocolate. The creamy white AF1, a hip-hop fashion classic, is made from the finest chocolate from Switzerland. Both special-edition shoes were reproduced in real-size, while the mini chocolate sneakers were made into VIP souvenirs.

ad.   *+41*
ph.   *+41*
pd.   *Bastien Thibault from Blondel*
cl.   *Nike*
y.   *2006, 2007*

   anniversary
         branding

*ChocolateAirForce1*AirForceTurns25Berlin

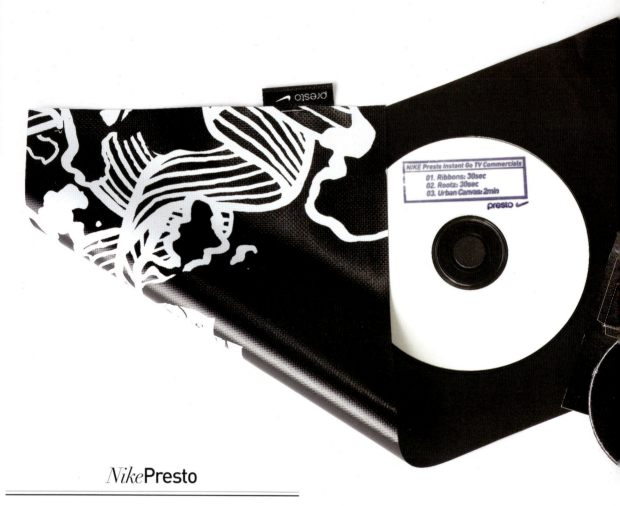

Nike **Presto**

The bouncing energy of urban street culture goes spontaneously with music, graffiti and extreme sports. Using the concrete jungle as background, Nike Presto expressed the "Instant go" spirit that goes with sports and spices up the backstreet. This black and white roll-up contains colorful goodies such as graffiti-art postcards, a miniature paper-folded DJ turntable, stickers and moving images flowing freely between the skyscrapers.

f. *Nike*
y. *2003*

 advertising

*NikePresto***InstantGo**

*Nike*JogaBonito

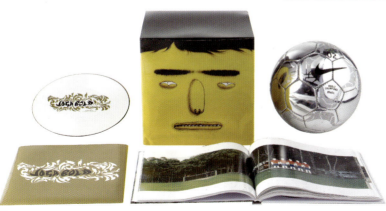

"Play Beautiful!" is what "Joga Bonito" means in Portuguese, and it all started in the football kingdom of Brazil. Pleasure and passion for the game is what makes its players beautiful, whether in the backstreets of Rio de Janeiro or on the world platform of an international stadium. The sports campaign's hardcover book introduces Brazilian football culture, street art and social portraits in vivid photographs, inviting readers, seekers and dreamers to journey through Brazil with this silver football souvenir.

f. Nike
y. 2006

advertising

*NikeAirMax360*FlashDrive

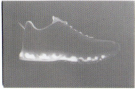

As the historical evolution of outstanding design can be traced through the design of the product itself, Nike has miniaturized its award-winning Air Max 360 model into a handy, pocket-sized, portable flash drive. But if the tangible object isn't enough, just pull it apart and plug it in to your computer's USB drive. Bridge the generation gap by storing all the retrospective info and more, in multimedia format.

f.   *Nike*
y.   *2006*

 product launch
advertising

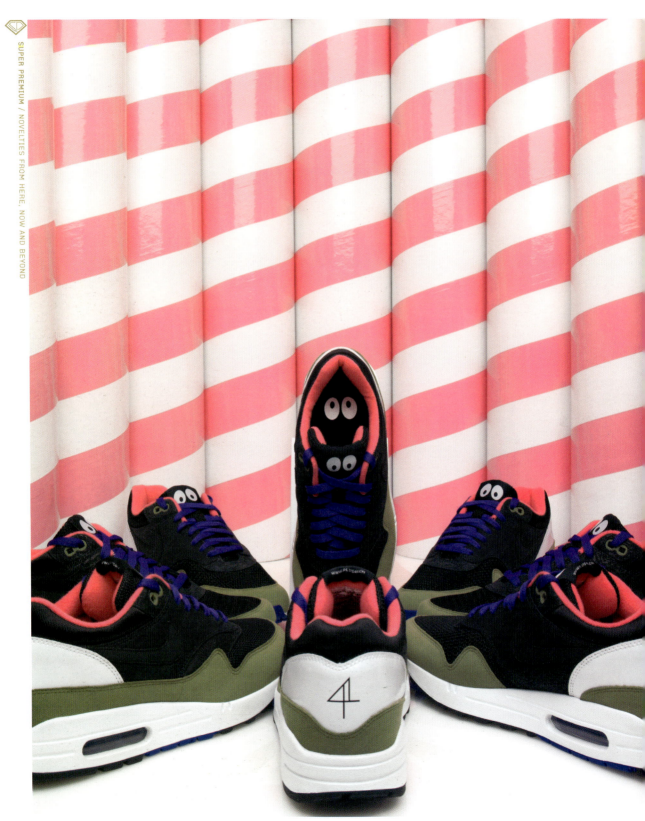

+41NikeiD AirMax1

Five exclusive googly-eyed pairs of Nike Air Max sneakers represented Nike's vision of Nike Air history. Not only do the eyes look back at you, they see a revolutionary system that introduced new techonology to the sneaker scene. All five pairs were auctioned at Thomas I Punkt shop in Hamburg, with all benefits going to Christie's.

ad.   +41
d.   +41
i.   +41
ph.   +41
cl.   Nike Germany
y.   2006
◈   *anniversary*

PUMA by MIHARAYASUHIRO

Puma MiharaYasuhiro

Reaching beyond the realms of both sports and fashion, Puma and Mihara work in collaboration to bring sportswear to another level of style. This paper fan souvenir and book of illustrations introduced the Japanese art collection of the Puma × Mihara Yasuhiro series, featuring original artworks transformed into decorative patterns on the shoes. Thus even sporty leather sneakers were considered as walking, running, jumping exhibitions of both fine art and tasteful fashion.

f.   PUMA
y.   2006-2007

 product launch

Dunhill/**Helmet**

Unveiling the first concept store in Asia in Beijing, Dunhill unfolded their swinging London spirits in their shop's grand opening. From the luxurious motorbikes parked outside to the limited-edition Dunhill medal and helmet offered to each guest, every detail of the Motorities Night Party embodied the spirit of motoring that Dunhill has maintained since its foundation.

f.   Dunhill
cl.   Dunhill
y.   2007

✂   *shop opening*

Bandeà Part Exhibition

The exhibition presents a cross-section of 10 photographers of the New York underground, from the late 1960s to the mid '80s, who were at the origin of the creative effervescence that shook the art, music and literary scenes. The opening souvenir was a pair of paper-folded speakers bearing novelty photos of rock, punk, hippie and disco themes, as pioneered by the exceptional artists of that era.

cl. *Agnès b. Librairie Galerie*
y. *2007*
CC *exhibition*

AnnDem HK1stAnniv.

Celebrating the first anniversary of Ann Demeulemeester's store in Hong Kong, the designer's signature sleek remanifests itself in black and white birthday party favors. The tote bag is numbered "1", while a pair of monochrome T-shirts suggest the letter "A" - for Ann and Anniversary - in the silhouetted form of a soldier at work. Each piece is wrapped with a black ribbon, tied with class like a satin sash.

y. *2007*
anniversary

ChingcameLight@MoeShinohara

ChingcameLight ⓐMoeShinohara

This handy flashlight literally projects the young and sexy image of the popular "Chingcame" photo series featured in the Japanese street fashion magazine for boys "smart". The Chingcame Light was a fun freebie attached to the magazine, which has been running the sexy photo series for over 10 years.

d.   *Rotar & Hideaki Naito*
ph. *Keisuke Naito [KiKi inc.]*
y.   *2007*

✺   *advertising*
♛   *branding*

Special thanks to Warner Bros. Entertainment Inc

*HarryPotter*PewterDragonEgg

Just as the boy wizard himself overcame the odds to obtain the precious Goblet of Fire, so Harry Potter fans must be deserving of this treasured miniature prize. The golden egg is engraved with the words "Chinese Fireball Dragon" and comes wrapped in a purple velvet pouch with golden tassel. Pull apart the two magnets holding the two halves of the egg together to hatch a delicately hand-sculpted and intricately detailed 6-centimeter pewter fireball dragon figurine.

f.　*Warner Bros Pictures Int'l*
y.　*2005*

　movie

MIHARAYASUHIRO

*SosuMiharaYasuhiro***Opening**

On August 25, Mihara Yasuhiro opened the first-ever overseas store in Hong Kong. To celebrate the moment, a retrospective exhibition and after-party took place on the eve, where gift sets were offered to every guest in a fake print paper bag, one of his famous tricks. Dig inside to discover the treats: a miniature shoe-horn keychain reminiscent of the designer's fine craftsmanship in footwear, and one vacuum-treated resin shoe pad, available in two sizes for men and women respectively. Of course, it takes two for a pair of shoes.

y.   SOSU MIHARAYASUHIRO
y.   2007

 new shop/company

JohnGallianoHomme **MosaicInvitation**

Fashion's enfant terrible John Galliano took inspiration from holy war and peace on this acrylic invitation to his S/S 08 fashion show. Following the "Apocalyptic Mayhem" theme, the plate is designed like a stained-glass mosaic replica of a guardian angel holding the flag leading us to peace.

y. 2007

 fashion show

*ArtVillageOsaki*GrowingGardener

In January 2007, the new Art Village Osaki was inaugurated east of Japan Railway's Osaki station. While the area includes both residential and office buildings, the town features a broad range of artworks installed within and around the premises. One of them is the Growing Gardener, which grew out of an original 16m-tall garden gnome, considered a guardian angel of the home. The Growing Gardener celebrates the grand opening of Art Village Osaki, as the town guardian loved by its people.

ad. *OBAYASHI CORPORATION (Japan)*
      Atelier G&B (Japan)
      NANJO and ASSOCIATES (Japan)
d.   *inges idee*
p.   *Maekawa Pro*
cl. *Art Village Osaki Urban Renewal Association*
      (Japan)
y.   *2007*

👑 *branding*

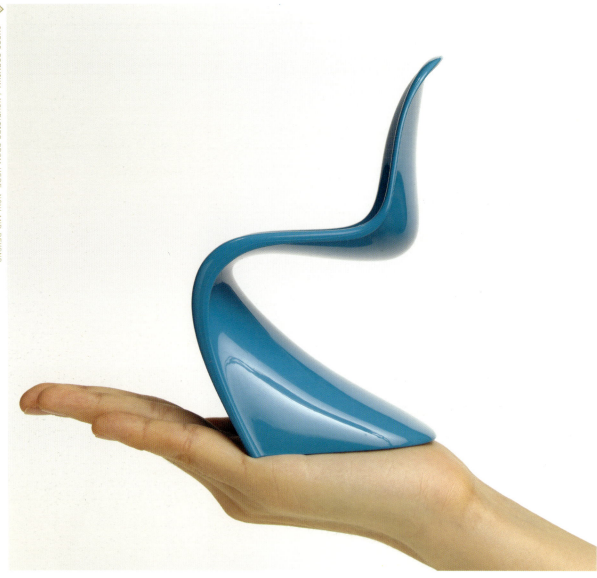

*Turquoise*PantonChairMiniature

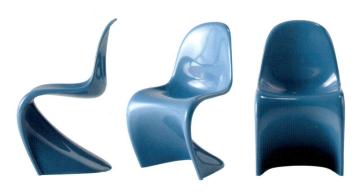

Verner Panton's cantilevered stacking chair was the first single-material and single-form chair to be made, following Vitra's three decades of investigation into plastic technology. The miniature model is as charming and finely crafted as the real thing in original turquoise blue - the theme color of hhstyle.com Aoyama. Celebrating the opening of hhstyle.com's new shop, this visual-tactile novelty in anti-proteolysis color is candy for the eye that fits comfortably in your palm.

f.   *hhstyle.com*
y.   *2004*

✂   *shop opening*

*AntonyChair*Miniature

The famous Anthony chair, which many connoisseurs regard as Prouvé's finest design, was miniaturized into a novelty gift for guests invited to the opening of hhstyle.com/sleep, as the shop's concept was "to enrich your private space". This highly detailed mini-model of the Vitra Design Museum's Miniatures Collection is an exact replica of the original, packaged in a simple wooden box, complete with brochure providing artistic and historical background, biography of the designer and production history of the featured chair.

f.   hhstyle.com
y.   2002

 new shop/company

ROCHAS

*PartC*LearnTheProcess

Examine the process of transformation from 2D to 3D

*Learn*How2Work

**KNOW HOW TO WORK A FLAT PAPER SKETCH
INTO A REAL-WORLD TOY**

p.206-211

*LearnThe*Stuff

**DIG INSIDE THE PROCESS OF STUFFING
A PLUSH BODY INTO A CUDDLY DOLL**

p.212-217

*LearnThe*Plastics

**DISCOVER THE TRICK OF MOLDING
FIGURES OUT OF PLASTIC MATERIAL**

p.218-221

*LearnThe*List

**EXAMINE THE A-Z OF PREMIUM CHOICES
FROM ECONOMY TO LUXURY**

p.222-227

NO MATTER HOW DIMENSIONAL YOUR VISION, YOU MUST FIRST SKETCH IT OUT
ON A PIECE OF PAPER OR IN A BLANK FILE. IT MAY EVEN BE A 3D DIAGRAM,
BUT IT IS STILL STUCK IN A 2D PLANE. FORTUNATELY THE 3D MASTERS CAN HELP YOU
LEAP THAT FINAL STRETCH FROM ORIGINAL DRAWING TO TANGIBLE ARTWORK.
MEET THE WIZARDS BEHIND THE MAGIC OF MODELING AND MOLDING.

Interview With **Howard** Lee

As the latest trend is making toy figures from artwork and comics, producing novelties often means selecting a single frame from the action, or a key angle in a series, and interpreting it into a real-life figurine. What is the secret to conserving the original's charm in a toy separated from its source? Let's see how "how2work" works it out.

"All along, Euro-American artists tend to be more hands-free and count on our expertise, while Hong Kong and Japanese artists are more persistent on every stage of the process, due to the fact that they know the workflow very well. When it comes to minute spacing, even so small as 1mm displacement, they will not settle for less."

When did you start designing art figures?
At the beginning, I was working in a comics studio, responsible for merchandise. Around 1999-2000, I worked with Hong Kong artist Michael Lau to produce the figure Tokyo Tribe. That was my very first time making a figure, and the experience sparked my interest in this profession. So in 2001 I decided to start my own studio focused on developing art figures and collaborating with artists and designers from around the world.

What makes art figures so special?
Many illustrators or comic artists' works are delivered on a 2D surface, while art figures translate these interesting works into a tangible 3D object in the real world. I think it offers a popular platform for the artwork to appear

in a more playful and friendly way, which in turn introduces the artist and artwork to a wider audience. 2D and 3D rebound off each other, enhance the original work, and enrich the artist and collectors, all of which is also what attracts me to be part of it.

Most of the artists with whom you have collaborated, such as Yoshitomo Nara and Santa Inoue, are keen on drawing. What is the process of transforming 2D into 3D?

First, the artist drafts an image of the desirable look, then we hand-carve an initial figure based on this draft. Both sides will refine this model until we all agree on an optimal design. Once the final model is confirmed, it is duplicated as a mold for production, following up with quality-check and final touch-up.

Generally we do extensive research on an artist's work, read almost all the books and imagery sources to get a thorough understanding of the artist's style. Transforming the style and essence of the artwork is not only technically challenging, it involves focus and attention to details, so the entire process demands more than just craftsmanship.

You have worked with many artists, both local and from overseas. What are the differences in working experiences?

Very often, overseas artists do not have a solid concept about the 2D-to-3D process. In their draft, they may draw a flat nose on the front view but indicate a tall nose on the side view, which produces a contradictory situation. Some artists from the U.S. and Europe prepare more drafts from different angles and postures, so that we can capture the best combination that presents the most desirable results from the images provided. On the other hand, Hong Kong artists are quite keen on sculpting and 3D modeling, so right from the start, they are very sure about each process and the details of how the transformation should be handled, which also gives the final product more unity.

❦ *Drawing and autograph of Nara Yoshitomo in the workinng table of How2Work Studio.* ❦ *Testing prototype of art figure Sleepless Night.* ❦ *Flocking is used for the clothes of Sleepless Night*

However, both local and overseas artists face problems during the production process, and unfortunately not all of them can compromise on the solutions. So our role is to balance both esthetic and practical needs with our knowledge and experience throughout the whole execution process.

All along, Euro-American artists tend to be more hands-free and count on our expertise, while Hong Kong and Japanese artists are more persistent on every stage of the process, due to the fact that they know the workflow very well. When it comes to minute spacing, even so small as 1mm displacement, they will not settle for less. That is quite a challenge, outside of the normal production routine. Looking back, it seems all these very little details are in delicate balance with the entire piece.

What other challenges do you encounter in the 2D-to-3D process?

I think each collaboration itself is already a challenge, because to be honest, nice work doesn't necessarily hook up to a good response on the market. Given that both the artist and our side devote so much in order to make it happen, we risk everything for what may come afterwards. And the utmost mentally challenging in the transformation process is how to communicate. It is not easy to convince the artist to accept adjustments that cater to the needs of production, prevailing yet conserving the essence of the design.

Another challenge is that over 60 percent of the production processes are handled manually, so the probability of human error is much higher. For us as designer and production manager, it is very important to check every step of the production, which is physically challenging.

In short, producers should be sharp and analytical toward audience tastes and market trends, in order to balance their judgment between artistic and market values.

Has there been any recent development in production techniques? How has it affected the final work?

Vinyl production, Fabric-Reinforced Polymeric (FRP) and small toys for Toei machine are the common variations of the figurine product – most notably, I would say, the 12" action figure. Nowadays, not only are designers and sculptors much more skillful, even collectors are able to appreciate the fine details. What they look for is a minimized version of the real world – the clothes, parts, all are a micro-reproduction of real life. I would say quality

❦ *Original sketch, testing dummy and facial-parts prototype of the character Hasheem of "Tokyo Tribe" for artist Santa Inoue.*

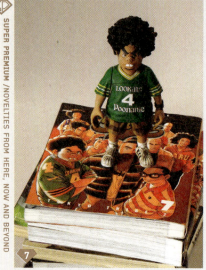

▼ *Final Hasheem figure, standing on comic-book reference "Tokyo Tribe"..*

on both the designer's side and the collector's side has risen a notch.

Developments in production techniques differ slightly among regions. Hong Kong is one of the top two that can convert 2D to the first working sample within three months; South Korean production is good at division of labor. Japanese production is well-knit with current trends, while Hong Kong keeps the balance between market value and good design.

Would you share your most unforgettable experience from your past collaborations?
Basically we highly appreciate all the artists with whom we collaborate. For the latest collaboration with artist Yoshitomo Nara on the art figure Sleepless Night, although we initiated the project three years ago, the whole project finally released early this year. We both prefered to discuss and develop the whole process face-to-face, yet due to Nara's traveling overseas and local exhibition tour, we had to keep in touch by long-distance, which was really not easy when discussing details. Glad that we were both happy with the end result.

8

9

Artists' original sketches and the ratio reference for final 3D figures.

Profile **Howard Lee**

Howard Lee founded How2Work in 2001 and has since been actively involved in artist collaborations for developing figures and original creations. His 3D collectibles include Sleepless Night for artist Yoshitomo Nara, Santastic!! series and Tokyo Tribe for artist Santa Inoue, and illustration book character series for illustrator Jimmy Liao. Other creations include Blue Smurf and Ashita no joe.

Interview With Saito

*In the wonderful world of premiums, no one can resist the soft touch of plush.
From the miniature trinket attached to the mobile strap to the meters-tall teddy
bear, about half of all souvenir gifts are cuddly plush toys. So how are flat line
drawings sewn up into tangible toy figures? Professionals from Saito provide a
full picture of the process from behind the scenes.*

①

②

When did you start designing soft toys? What is your role?

We have been making stuffed and plush toys ever since the 1980s, for clients such as Sanrio and artists such as Hayao Miyazaki. Clients or creators provide us with a 2D draft, then our designers and sewist calculate the proportion from the 2D design and begin the production process.

What is the work flow for the whole production process?

Once we receive the design from our client, our designers print out the draft and start calculating the 3D structure. We begin with the head, then the main body and all the other parts are deduced into different paper patterns. As the 3D surfaces form optical illusions, the designers and sewist must fine-tune the patterns to achieve the desired results. For example, if there are lots of curvatures and pointy shapes in the 3D, the patterns must be slightly enlarged to achieve a visual balance.

❸ *Documentation of each product's materials.* ❹ *Calculation of paper pattern ratio based on 2D photo reference.* ❺ *First draft of paper pattern according to the photo of a teddy bear.* ❹ *Plush samples for materials matching.* ❺ *Library of cloth and fur.*

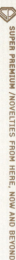

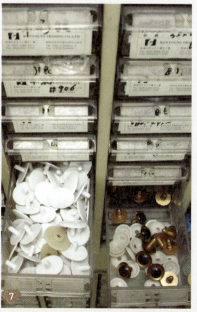

❤ *Library of threads sorted by color, thickness and texture.* ❤ *Index and sample library of push button parts – for eyes, noses, body joints and apparel accessories.*

After sketching out all the patterns, the designer marks all the details of the sewing sequence, matching the color and materials according to the client's request. The designer picks out the optimal combination and other possible variations from the materials library and passes the patterns and materials to the sewist to handmake the first sample.

Once the first sample is finished, the designer and project manager discuss the results internally, then send to the client for approval. Taking into account the client's comments, the designer adjusts and amends the sample by hand before returning it to the client. Most often the adjustments are very minor, so one designer will be dedicated to following every step of a project. If the client is satisfied with the results, mass production begins.

What difficulties do you encounter throughout the entire production process?

Although more than half of our clients only provide one view of their design, our designers and sewist can deduce and design the all-round shapes from the draft, as they all are very experienced in reconstructing the form and structure. Indeed, the complexity of production workflow depends on the details and combination of materials in the design.

Details and parts account for only a very small proportion of the finished product, but they are the crucial points that give soul to the figure. It requires a technical, but also quite subjective, perception that is not easy to explain. Once we were requested to design a plush in the form of an angel, and we revised six to seven times, which is quite rare, as it took so many times to refine. Finally we understood that the client wanted a smooth and seamless surface for the angel's baby face, so we totally changed the structure and materials. We used hot-stamping and silk-screen printing to create a round face and limbs, and our client was happy with the result.

And changes in materials affect the fundamental elements of the structure. For example, if we change the main body materials from cotton cloth to swimsuit cloth, then the whole structure, parts details and paper patterns need to be completely redesigned. Because there is a big difference in elasticity between these two materials, the same pattern used to make the figure in swimsuit cloth would be too loose and lose its form. In addition, changes in body materials require more

than simply rematching the detailed parts, so finally it takes more time to make the sample. So any change to the main body material in the middle of the design process is quite tricky.

From paper to finishing the first sample, how long does it take?

Generally, taking a six-inch-tall stuffed toy as an example, designing the structure and patterns takes two to three days; materials matching and adjustment takes two to three days; handmaking the sample takes about four to five days. So the whole process takes about 10 to 15 days to complete. But it depends on the complexity of the figure's structure.

As materials matching is so crucial, are there any special precautions or rules?

It is mainly determined by the size of the final product. For small hand-size toys, it is better to use shorter fluff such as terry cloth, polyester fabric and velvet with fluffs under 6mm, which can present cleaner, more refined forms for the design. Bigger plush toys are better adapted to long-fluff materials for a softer image.

Do you find any common misinterpretations or difficulties during the production and design?

There is a misunderstanding that small plush parts like doll ornaments for mobile straps are low in production cost. Actually, the smaller the size, the more attention to details is necessary.

Implanting electronic parts is difficult, as these parts are tricky to adjust and repair. 3D toys based on the image of a real person are especially challenging, as it is not easy to minimize the features of the original image while keeping its essence.

Has any recent technological development in materials introduced changes to your designs?

For the technique, we now use laser to cut out patterns as small as 1.5mm in diameter. Laser can also be used for eroding patterns on the cloth as part of the fabric design, thus creating a lace effect for the details. In recent years there has been an impressive development in materials. Before we basically used cotton, leather, plastic buttons and velvet; nowadays, we have the choice of thin transparent materials, metallic fabrics and heat-sensitive (color-changing) materials. And parts components such as lace, ribbons and crystal ornaments also provide a wide range of options for new designs.

❦ *Each model is documented with an individual record including all paper patterns, materials used and refinements.* ❦ *Sewist cutting clothes for hand samples.*

1. Beginning with a sketch from the client, the designer calculates measurements and drafts patterns for the figure.

2. The designer matches appropriate body materials and parts.

3. The sewist then draws paper patterns on different materials accordingly.

4. & 5. Materials are then cut into the appropriate shapes, and the sewist hand-sews the first sample for the client's approval.

StuffedToys

Given the popularity of stuffed toys, there exists a wide range of stuffing materials to cater to all desires: fabric-cottons for a bouncy, soft-touch, weighted plastic beans for extra texture, or goose feathers for a loose, light body. In many cases, various materials are mixed and stuffed together – for example, feathers for the main body and beans for the paws and buttocks. While the production of stuffed toys is highly modernized, the end-product still depends very much on manpower and craftsmanship to design the fusion of materials and sewing details into the refined figure of a beloved character.

6. Once the first hand sample is made, the designer and sewist may have additional suggestions for the finishing. All these materials are sent to the client for final confirmation and approval.

Interview With ManMing

Besides plush, the other half of premium gifts are produced by injection molding of hard plastic. From mini-figurines inside crystal balls to 12-inch action figures with 40 joints, professionals from Man Ming explain the wide range of plastic molding techniques used to translate 2D surfaces into 3D sculptures.

"As a designer and probably the investor of the design, it is essential to plan very carefully before going into a production involving lots of refinement and modeling. For plastic modeling, it takes at least two to three months to complete the whole production, so if the design targets a volatile trend, the final product might be outdated by the time it is actually produced."

Generally, what materials do you use to make plastic products?

There are two materials that are commonly used to make plastic figures and models: one is Poly-Vinyl Chloride (PVC) and the other is Acrylonitrile-Butadiene Styrene (ABS). PVC has been widely used over the past 30 years, so the production technique is well developed. PVC is elastic, which allows for more accuracy when making bigger models or figures with more curvatures. While ABS is relatively new, it has the advantage of finer particles, which offer a delicate surface and more color availability. ABS is usually used for making fine parts and miniatures – even parts as small as 5mm can be injected with patterns.

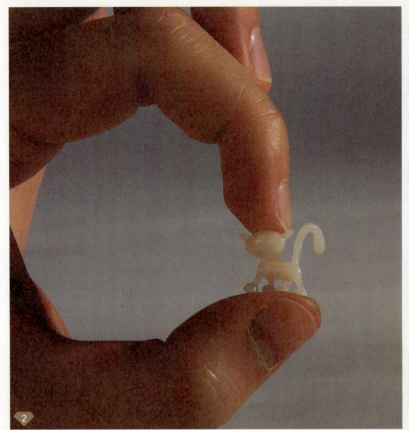

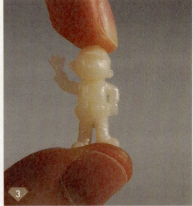

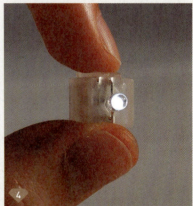

What is the workflow for producing a plastic figure?

Everything starts with the flat surface. The client provides drafts with at least one to six views of their end-product, so our sculptor can hand-shape the 3D figure with oil clay. Generally it takes 10 to 14 days to transform 2D graphics into 3D models. This handmade model is then duplicated with soft plastic paste and sent to the client for approval. If there are comments and requests for refinement, the sculptor adjusts the oil clay model accordingly. This process is repeated until the desirable result is achieved, with each refinement taking seven to ten days to complete.

After confirming the model, we digitize the shape and engrave the mold for injection, then we inject the figures and color them one by one. In short, the whole production process takes around three months to complete.

Why are some plastic figures hollow, while others are not?

This is a production method that depends on the size and structure of the final product. During the production process, a plastic solution is injected into the copper mold. If the container is large, the injected liquid flows into the mold and leaves traces on the surface of the model once it solidifies.

To resolve this problem, we deconstruct the design into small parts, turning the massive solid body into several conjoined hollow parts. While this method prevents flow scars on the surface by producing a relatively thinner case, it requires more pre-production work for the designer, who must calculate the parts and structure, as well as post-production composition after modeling. So finally this method requires much more time and cost.

Have there been any significant technological developments for designing plastic figures?

Digitizing and 3D scanning now provide designers with a very detailed design on screen. Unlike the artisanal handcrafted method, any resizing can be done easily on the computer, and it can rectify small defects such as asymmetrical shapes. It really saves time and improves accuracy, as these digital models can be directly outputted to make the injection mold.

Are there any special precautions for designers during the plastic modeling process?

There are three main precautions that should be taken as a designer and producer. At the production level, the fewer the connection joints, the bigger the risk of displacing the

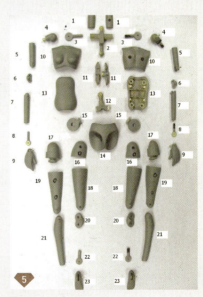

▼ *Pairs of injection molds for three figures' heads.* ▼▼▼ *4mm-tall miniature and electronic parts using ABS for injection molding.* ▼ *Action-figure parts modeled with ABS plastic injection.*

HowItLevelsUp
ProcessOfPlasticFigureMolding

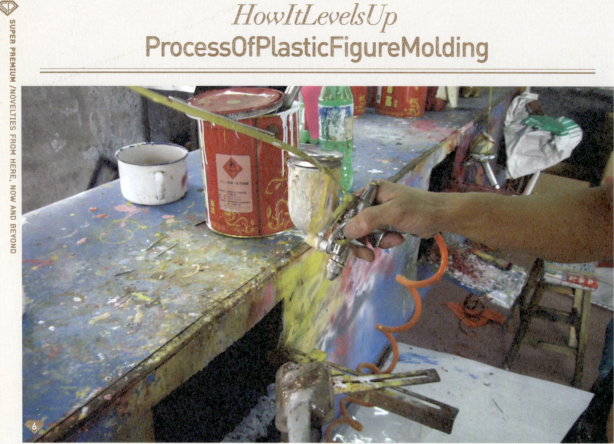

❤ *Most 3D figures are colored by airbrush, and each material (PVC or ABS) must be painted with its corresponding paint to avoid decoloring. In this photo, workers color by airbrush in front of an exhaust tube.*
❤ *Stainless- steel blocks before engraving onto injection molds.* ❤ *Engraving with electronic drills.*

composition. It is much more difficult to calculate the deconstruction of large-size end-products with complicated 3D parts and curvatures, which means a higher risk of defects. Second, designers should never neglect the safety check, which is crucial for the product's success on the market. Because of varying safety standards around the world, testing and certification takes around two to three weeks. It is best to communicate with your production manager so that he or she can check the areas of distribution in advance, and thus prevent unexpected delays in return.

Last but not least, as a designer and probably the investor of the design, it is essential to plan very carefully before going into a production involving lots of refinement and modeling. For plastic modeling, it takes at least two to three months to complete the whole production, so if the design targets a volatile trend, the final product might be outdated by the time it is actually produced..

♦♦Tailor-made copper mask clips are used to cover the rest of the figure when coloring different parts.
♦ Coloring masks used for coloring a single 3cm plastic figure with 4 colors.

LearnTheProducts
PremiumProductsForAllOccasions

A plush doll for an opening? A push pin for an exhibtion? No matter what, when and where the occasion, all the above and any of the unexpected novelties are always a welcome delight. Every aspect of your souvenir item influences the design and affects your choice of materials for the final product. This appendix of common premium gifts offers noteworthy tips and practical references of time and cost, as well as a few alternative twists.

◆ *Tee*

- **EXAMPLE** Cotton T-shirt with 4-color silk-screen printing, printing area 60cm x 45cm, back and front printable

- **COMMON APPLICATION** Promotion crew uniforms, novelty gifts for event launch, concert

- **PRODUCTION INFO**
- **MOQ** : 100 pcs
- **Unit Price** : Approx. US$ 4.5
- **Production Time** :
  Sampling → 10-14 days;
  mass production → 30-45 days

♥ **NOTES!**

- T-shirt color, cut and material variable

- Silk-screen and other printing effects such as foil hot-sampling, photo ink-jet printing, flocking and embroidery available

- Besides the back and front body areas of the tee, tage and labels can also be custom designed

◆ *Button badge*

- **EXAMPLE** 55mm diameter, 4-color printed, gloss lamination, iron back and pin

- **COMMON APPLICATION** Freebies for magazines, advertising campaigns, music concerts

- **PRODUCTION INFO**
- **MOQ** : 3000 pcs
- **Unit Price** : Approx. US$ 0.3
- **Production Time** :
  Sampling → 7-14 days;
  mass production → 21-25 days

♥ **NOTES!**

- Also available in 20mm, 25mm, 30mm, 40mm and 50mm diameters

- Emboss, deboss effects and cloth-mount also available

- Stainless-steel back and pin can also be used to make more durable

- Besides graphics and illustrations, photos can be printed on badge

◆ Pin

- **EXAMPLE** 2-color hard enamel pin, 25mm x 30mm die-cut shape

- **COMMON APPLICATION** Club member badge, anniversary memento

- **PRODUCTION INFO**
- **MOQ** : 500 pcs
- **Unit Price** : US$0.7-1;
  *set-up charge → US$350-400
- **Production Time** :
  Sampling → 7-14 days;
  mass production → 21-25 days

♥ **NOTES!**

- Injection die-cast can provide a 3D surface with antique metallic finish

- Contrary to injection molding, stamping can offer depressed graphic etching

- Epoxy, screen-printing, offset printing, PVC with 2D or 3D cast also available for finish

- Cost depends on number of colors used and surface area of pin

◆ Mug

- **EXAMPLE** diameter 65mm x 80mm tall porcelain mug with 2-color silk-screen printed design

- **COMMON APPLICATION** Thank-you gift for customers, company novelty

- **PRODUCTION INFO**
- **MOQ** : 3000 pcs
- **Unit Price** : US$3.5
  *mold charge US$1200
- **Production Time** :
  mold production → 30 days
  mass production → 30 days

♥ **NOTES!**

- Pad-printing transfers fine graphic details, suitable for image or photo printing

- Tailor-made modeling available for customized shape design

- Temperature-sensitive coating becomes transparent when mug contains hot or cold liquid, offers layering design for graphic print

◆ Candle

- **EXAMPLE** Scented candle in glass cup, diameter 60mm x 80mm tall, 1-color print

- **COMMON APPLICATION** Opening gift, exhibition gift

- **PRODUCTION INFO**
- **MOQ** : 500 pcs
- **Unit Price** : US$ 1-1.5
- **Production Time** :
  Sampling → 7-10 days;
  mass production → 25-30 days

♥ **NOTES!**

- Safety precaution note required for flammable goods

- Scent variable

- Besides glass, jar and container-free candles also available for finishing

- Candle-art and tailor-made sculpting service with candles also available for small-quantity orders

◆ *Tote bag*

- **EXAMPLE** 200mm x 300mm with handle, 200g/m² cotton cloth, 1-color print

- **COMMON APPLICATION** Shopping bag for fashion boutique or food shop, novelty gift packaging

- **PRODUCTION INFO**
- MOQ : 500 pcs
- Unit Price : US$2
  *set-up charge → US$350-400
- Production Time :
  sampling → 7 days
  mass production → 20-25 days

♥ **NOTES!**

- Nylon, PVC (polyvinyl chloride, soft plastic), leather and PU (polyurethane, supplement for leather) can also be used

- Silk-screen printing, embroidery and PVC lamination finishing on cotton bag are common

- Parts or accessories such as key rings and mobile straps can be attached to constitute a promotional set

- Tote bag itself can be used to package other promotional objects

◆ *Key Chain*

- **EXAMPLE** 15mm x 20mm metal charm with 40mm diameter steel ring

- **COMMON APPLICATION** Company novelty, advertising campaign grip-to-bag freebie, light thank-you gift

- **PRODUCTION INFO**
- MOQ : 500 pcs
- Unit Price : US$1
  *set-up charge US$300
- Production Time :
  mold production → 10-14 days
  mass production → 18-21 days

♥ **NOTES!**

- Key chain can also be used as mobile-phone strap

- Production varieties similar to *pin, changeable parts can be combined

- Electronic components such as flashlights, image projectors and mini torch-parts can be combined to include promotion information

- Electronic gadgets such as USB flash drives can be added to key chain for multi-media promotion details

◆ *Toilet-paper roll*

- **EXAMPLE** 30m, 1-color print with 1-color print paper wrap

- **COMMON APPLICATION** New medium for corporate branding, can also carry messages, slogans, introductions

- **PRODUCTION INFO**
- MOQ : 50,000 rolls
- Unit Price : US$0.8; US$250 color print (on tissue)
- Production Time :
  30-35 days

♥ **NOTES!**

- Available in packs of 2, 4, 6, 8, 10 and 12 rolls, in PVC bag or mounted with shrink wrap

- 1- or 2-color print available for pattern

- Pattern's maximum designable length is 25cm, repeats as monogram for rest of roll

◈ *Tissue pack*

- **EXAMPLE** PVC pack of 15 tissues, 70mm x 100mm, 2-color print

- **COMMON APPLICATION** Hand-out freebies for roadside promotion, commonly distributed with inserted leaflet for promotion details

- **PRODUCTION INFO**
- **MOQ** : 10,000 pcs
- **Unit Price** : US$0.07; *US$100 / color print (on package)
- **Production Time :** 15 days

♥ **NOTES!**
- Besides PVC wrap, small paper box offers more printable area on package
- QC control with hygiene certification required
- Tissues can be printed with logo or campaign image endorsement
- Extra cost involved for QC control

◈ *Paper Matches*

- **EXAMPLE** 40mm x 50mm x 5mm, 1-color print

- **COMMON APPLICATION** Hotel, bar, restaurant and shop freebies

- **PRODUCTION INFO**
- **MOQ** : 5,000 pcs
- **Unit Price** : US$0.5
- **Production Time** : 20-25 days

♥ **NOTES!**
- Small sizes: 2" x 1" box, 2" x 3" tube and triangle box
- Color of match head variable
- Safety precaution note appear on the product
- Paper box and tube offer more printable areas for graphics and promotional information

◈ *USB flash drive*

- **EXAMPLE** 1GB USB flash drive in PU case with hot-stamp

- **COMMON APPLICATION** Event opening, advertising campaign, wedding and anniversary party

- **PRODUCTION INFO**
- **MOQ** : 100 pcs
- **Unit Price** : US$35
- **Production Time :** 14-20 days (USB) 20 days (PU case)

♥ **NOTES!**
- Multi-media promotions such as movie trailers, documents and images can be pre-loaded into memory
- QC check and warranty required for electronic appliance
- Case of USB drive can be customized with different tailor-made casts; longer production time required for mold set-up and inlay of USB parts

◈ *Plush Doll*

- **EXAMPLE** 120mm x 120mm x 60mm plush doll in 6mm fake fur

- **COMMON APPLICATION** Redemption of purchase or thank-you gift

- **PRODUCTION INFO**
- MOQ : 1000 pcs
- Unit Price : US$3
  *set-up charge → US$350-400
- Production Time :
  sampling → 14 days
  mass production → 45 days

♥ **NOTES!**

- Safety precaution note must be attached to product itself

- Certification of safety test required to ensure final product is needle-free

- Mini-size plush can be attached to mobile-phone strap, can also be combined with wide range of lifestyle goods such as tote bags and tissue boxes

◈ *Inflatable Doll*

- **EXAMPLE** 180mm x 90mm, 0.25mm thick PVC, 1-color print

- **COMMON APPLICATION** Freebie for exhibition opening and advertising campaign

- **PRODUCTION INFO**
- MOQ : 1000 pcs
- Unit Price : US$0.7
- Production Time :
  mold production → 7-14 days
  mass production → 30 days

♥ **NOTES!**

- Safety precaution note must be attached to product itself

- Mini-size doll can be attached to mobile-phone strap

- Inflatable toys are mainly produced with Polyvinyl-Chloride(PVC), Polypropylene (PP) or soft plastic, which under high-tempatures (40ºC) may melt or produce a peculiar smell. For inflatable objects intended for outdoor use, it is preferable to manufacture the figure out of thin nylon cloth instead of plastic

◈ *Ball-point Pen*

- **EXAMPLE** 1-color pen with 1-color silk-screen print

- **COMMON APPLICATION** Bank and insurance company novelty, concert freebie

- **PRODUCTION INFO**
- MOQ : 1000 pcs
- Unit Price : US$0.35
- Production Time :
  14 days

♥ **NOTES!**

- Besides silk-screen printing, laser engraving is also commonly used for graphic treatment

- A rolled mini leaflet or flat paper calendar can unscroll from the body of the pen

- Pen can be combined with other mini stationery such as memo stickies and correction belts for multi-function use

*Production*Glossary!

Notes are never sufficient for numerous communications with your production crew and partners. From pre-production quantity check, product testing and logistic arrangements, to adaptation and refinement throughout the creative process, to final approval and follow-up, knowing how to express the tech-specs and professional codes will give you the fluency and efficiency to realize your dream.

Technical terms for those in-the-know:

• FOB
Free on Board / Freight on Board

The seller pays for transportation on board. It also implies that the seller is responsible for the safety of the goods until they are handed over to the buyer.

• MOQ
Minimum Order Quantity

The "Minimum Order Quantity" check on the production order is very important, as it varies from product to product.

• QC
Quality Control

A checking team that ensures the stability of the final products. QC check is crucial for any production, and a reliable QC team helps to prevent a high rate of defects.

• OEM
Original Equipment Manufacturer

Refers to a situation in which one company purchases a manufactured product from another company and resells the product as its own. This production flow saves time in product development and is widely used for producing novelty goods.

• ODM
Original Design Manufacturer

The Original Design Manufacturer is a company which manufactures a product that will ultimately be branded by another firm for sale. Often adopted in international trade where a local ODM is used to produce goods for a foreign company.

• MOLDS
For tailor-made modeling / designs

The mold is the hollow form that gives a particular shape to molten or plastic. Also known as injection molding, as it is widely used in plastic modeling of both soft and hard plastic products. Generally takes two to three months to produce tailor-made molds.

• ISO
International Organization for Standardization

An international standard-setting body composed of representatives from various national-standard bodies and some government boards providing worldwide industrial and commercial standards. Certifications approved by ISO mean the product meets the authorities' required standards.

• SAMPLING
Testing for the final product

A small number of products intended to show the quality or the combination of final designs. Sampling time may be extended due to refinements and testing results, so it is important to pre-check to avoid unexpected delays.

• WARRANTY
Remedy for defection

An obligation that an article or service sold is as factually stated or legally implied by the seller, and that often provides a specific remedy such as repair or replacement in the event the article or service fails to meet the warranty. Warranty service is especially important for products with electronic parts.

* Cost and conditions may vary according to raw materials, techniques and production conditions in different regions.

Super Premium
Novelties from here and beyond

Creative & Editorial Direction
AllRightsReserved

Associate Producer
Janet Lui (AllRightsReserved)

Contributing Editor
Taka Nakanishi

Japanese Coordinator
Etsuko Yoshizawa

Copywriter
Cherise Fong

Art Director
AllRightsReserved, Godfrey Kwan (junkiedesign)

Designer
AllRightsReserved, Godfrey Kwan (junkiedesign)

Photographer
Myke Cheng

Special Thanks
Winifred Lai, Joanne Cheung, Stephanie Au, John Leung

First Published in 2007 by AllRightsReserved Ltd.
tel: (852) 27120873 fax: (852) 27126701 url: www.allrights-reserved.com

For General Enquires
info@allrights-reserved.com

For Distribution
garylau@allrights-reserved.com

For Editorial Submission & Collaborations
editor@allrights-reserved.com

Printed In Hong Kong
ISBN 978-988-99001-5-1

*Contributors'***Profiles**

Contributors' Profiles

+41

//DIY (Do It Yourself) is a graphic design studio founded in 2001 by Laurence Jaccottet, Philippe Cuendet and Ivan Liechi. One of the main objectives of //DIY is to create a multi-disciplinary platform focused on graphic design. Since creating their own fashion brand +41, they have collaborated with brands such as Nike, Etnies Plus, NSL, 242. They have also expanded their talent to music publishing via +41 recordings.

url www.plus41.ch
www.diy.li

1LOVE

AIR FORCE 1 ONLY SHOP opened in Harajuku, Tokyo, in celebration of the 25th anniversary of AIR FORCE 1 – the one-year collaboration project of NIKE X realmadHECTIC.

url nike1love.jp

A.T

Established in Japan in 1982 by founder and creative director Atsuro Tayama, A.T is a young label with strong artistic qualities and a taste of French avant-garde at modest pricing, designed according to the key concept of neo classic. A.T also suggests "to mix and not to match", encouraging the wearer to create their individual persona without being bound by trends.

AllRightsReserved

AllRightsReserved is a Hong Kong-based creative studio established in 2003 with the belief that design unleashes the possibilities of synthesizing various media, where concepts bounce off craftsmanship to broaden the horizon for creative solutions.

url www.allrights-reserved.com

Agnès b.

Agnès b. opened her first store on Rue du Jour in Paris in 1975. This area served as her office and studio but was also a place for self-expression and encounters. Since then the company has opened more than a hundred stores worldwide. Art occupies an important place in the life and work of Agnès b. In 1984 she opened the Galerie du Jour, and in 1997 she established the film production company Lovestreams Productions Agnès b.

url agnesb.com

Antoine+Manuel

Antoine Audiau and Manuel Warosz met in art school in Paris. They quickly decided to work together under the name Antoine+Manuel, combining hand drawing and computer illustration with their personal typography and photography. They have worked in fashion (Christian Lacroix), home (Habitat, Galeries Lafayette), publishing (Larousse), contemporary dance, theater and art.

e c@antoineetmanuel.com
url www.antoineetmanuel.com

Arc

Arc Worldwide delivers total marketing solutions to connect consumers, brands and channels. ARChitectureTM, its strategic-planning process, fuses content and contact to create profitable brand experiences. Key disciplines include Retail Marketing, Public Relations, CRM and Direct Marketing, Events and Promotions, and Digital Interactive.

url www.arcww.com

BEAMS

BEAMS was established in 1976 with an "unwavering goal to be a contributing force in society", manifested in its Tokyo-ist mission to be the cultural and commercial pulse of fashion and lifestyle trends in Japan. Thirty years later, the group is composed of three complementary and collaborative organizations, which manufacture, wholesale and retail imported clothing, original-brand clothing and sundry goods. Its most recent division, BEAMS CREATIVE, is responsible for research and development, planning, execution and promotional activities, as well as music production and printing.

url www.beams.co.jp

Bucci

Founded by art director Nakashiro Takuya in 2007, Bucci focuses on art direction and graphic design for projects such as music packaging and fashion advertising.

butterfly stroke inc.

Since its establishment in 1999, butterfly-stroke inc. has been primarily involved in the creative side of advertising. The company's management and licensing division was established in January 2003 to manage artists and their creations, including character licensing, merchandise planning and production, as well as sales. Creative designers, who work under contract, develop a total character concept, which includes the creation of the character, its background and related merchandise.

url www.butterfly-stroke.com

CIBONE

Cibone is a lifestyle store with two locations (Aoyama and Jiyugaoka) in Tokyo, Japan. It proffers "superior design, unlimited by constraints of the imagination, beyond era and style for the people who know authenticity. Free style remixing for total living... art, music, interior and fashion edited to perfection. Creating a pleasurable experience for everyone."

url www.cibone.com

Diesel

The Diesel brand was founded by Renzo Rosso in 1978, and has since grown into an international design company, manufacturing jeans and casual clothing, as well as accessories. It is present in over 80 countries with over 5,000 points of sale and more than 300 mono-brand stores. Diesel launched its own Web site in 1995 and entered the world of e-commerce in 1997, selling jeans online in Finland and Sweden. The now famous Diesel advertising campaigns started in 1991 are characterized by a single creative execution run in every market of the world.

url www.diesel.com

Dunhill

The history of Alfred Dunhill began in the hands of a young entrepreneur and inventor in the late 19th century. As he took over the family saddlery business on Euston Road in London in 1893 at the age of 21, Alfred's stewardship coincided with the dawn of the motorcar. Today, Alfred Dunhill has over 180 stores around the world selling menswear, leather goods, men's jewelry, writing instruments, timepieces, gifts and games.

url www.dunhill.com

Harbour City

Situated in the commercial hub of Tsim Sha Tsui, Harbour City is Hong Kong's largest shopping and entertainment center, with a total area of 2 million square feet, including over 700 shops, 50 restaurants and two cinemas. Among its four major zones are the many flagship boutiques on Canton Road, which showcases an exclusive range of fashion and lifestyle shops. Performances and exhibitions are regularly hosted at the complex, while its "Music in the City" program attracts thousands of shoppers and tourists each weekend.

url www.harbourcity.com.hk

hhstyle.com

Established in 2000, hhstyle.com is an interior design and lifestyle shop inspired by the "hh" (hundred happenings) of its name, which represents its concept: "hhstyle.com is a place where you can discover your own lifestyle, so please see and select a product with 100 values, not just one."

url www.hhstyle.com

Kazunari Hattori

Born in Tokyo in 1964. After working for Light Publicity, he went freelance in 2001. Major works include art direction for Kewpie Corporation, Kirin Brewery, Parco and East Japan Railway; art direction for Ryuko Tsushin and Here and There magazines; package design for Otsuka Pharmaceutical; graphic design for an exhibition at Yokohama Museum of Art and book design for Ohunsha dictionaries.

FLAME, inc.

FLAME, inc. was founded in 2001 by art director and graphic designer Masayoshi Kodaira, who is active in a wide range of project areas, including graphic, advertising, editorial, CI and sign design. A member of the Tokyo Type Director's Club (Tokyo TDC), his awards include four Distinctive Merits from The Art Directors Club, New York and a New Designer Award from the Japan Graphic Designers Association (JAGDA).

groovisions

Groovisions is a Tokyo-based design group led by Hiroshi Ito that manages a wide range of projects including graphic design, promotional video, sound installation, fashion design and production work for global companies such as Nike. Groovisions has also been featured in international exhibitions, including "SuperFlat", curated by Takashi Murakami, and "JAM" in London, while a selection of its work has been presented at Colette in Paris. Groovisions is best known for the Chappie character, one among many products showcased in an original store in Tokyo.

url www.groovisions.com

MaisonMartinMargiela

Martin Margiela founded Maison Martin Margiela with Jenny Meirens in Paris in 1988. In 2000, their first shop opened in Tokyo, followed by Brussels, Paris, Aoyama, Osaka and London. Martin Margiela is considered a conceptual fashion artist. In his collections themes such as the reproduction of materials and the deconstruction of patterns and shapes are often interwoven. He uses both garments from flea markets and new pieces, taking them apart to subsequently reassemble them and create unique items. As a protest against the fashion world, Margiela uses veiled models on the catwalk and empty white labels to identify his creations.

url www.maisonmartinmargiela.com

Maria Luisa

The first Maria Luisa boutique opened its doors at 2 rue Cambon in Paris in 1988. Maria Luisa Poumaillou says: "Luxury is a state of mind not a brand; it is about freedom, rarity, exclusiveness and style. In a world where it has become a mass-market affair and where prices are often more related to packaging and advertising than to exquisite craftsmanship, I truly believe there is room for a small niche of difference. My selection is a very personal one, which makes the Maria Luisa concept like a private little club of friendly happy few."

url www.marialuisaboutique.com

mint designs

mint designs is a fashion brand created by Hokuto Katsui and Nao Yagi in Tokyo in 2001. mint designs joined Tokyo Collections after presenting its 2003 Spring-Summer collection. Katsui and Yagi, as the design unit, have recently extended their creative design beyond fashion to various other fields of art.

url www.mint-designs.com

Naomi Hirabayashi

Born in Tokyo in 1968, Naomi Hirabayashi graduated from the Department of Scenography, Display and Fashion design of Musashino Art University in 1992. Afterward she worked in Shiseido's advertising department, before becoming a freelance designer. Recently she participated in the group exhibition "Graphic Wave 2006" with art directors Masayoshi Kodaira, Manabu Mizuono and Eiji Yamada.

NTT DoCoMo

NTT DoCoMo is Japan's leading mobile communications operator. With over 51 million subscribers as of March 2006, DoCoMo accounts for more than half of Japan's mobile-phone market and has one of the largest subscriber bases of any mobile-phone company in the world. Established in July 1992 to take over the mobile-communications business of Nippon Telegraph and Telephone Corporation (NTT), NTT DoCoMo launched its first digital cellular-phone service in 1993.

url www.nttdocomo.co.jp

Paperlux

Paperlux is dedicated to "the finest impression on paper", in both product packaging and corporate design. It has developed a unique finishing process patented by Paperlux TM in Europe, which clears away the upper layer of the material, while the back remains unaffected. A relief formation brings the print alive in three-dimensional signatures and pictures.

url www.paperlux.com

Paul & Joe

Named after French fashion designer Sophie Albou's two sons, Paul & Joe was launched in 1995. After the success of Albou's men's collection, Albou was asked to design a women's collection. In 2003, Paul & Joe diversified to include cosmetics, and today it has 30 flagship stores worldwide, including four London boutiques owned by the Metta family.

url www.paulandjoe.com

Ports 1961

Originating in Canada under the direction of Mr. Luke Tanabe, Ports International launched its first collection in 1961. From the beginning, Ports was built on manufacturing luxury clothing, expanding the business to North America, Europe and Asia. Fine craftsmanship, expert tailoring and superior fabrics are the cornerstones of the Ports 1961 identity. The Ports 1961 lifestyle is driven by real-world needs as well as old-world romance.

url www.ports1961.com

Power Graphixx

Power Graphixx is a design team established in 1996 in Tokyo, Japan. Power Graphixx has been working on printed media, Web design and motion graphics for advertising campaigns, editorial designs, logo designs, CD sleeves, opening titles for TV, event movies, music videos, etc. Their main clients are Konami, Space Shower TV and Uniqlo.

url www.power-graphixx.com

Q-pot

Founded by 30-year-old designer Tadaaki Wakamatsu in 2002, Q-pot believes that dialogue and communication can make world peace. Q-pot products are designed to be a communication tool that leads to dialogue between people. Q-pot has three shop locations in Tokyo, including a gallery/shop opened in 2004. Q-pot is partial to sweets; in 2007 he designed a Special Chocolate Collection featuring jewelry and accessories made from chocolate bars, truffles and strawberries with whipped cream.

url www.gramme.jp

Sally Scott

Sally Scott is the brand based on the imaginary character, who is pure, curious, and always exploring new aspects of herself. The theme of each season reflects a part of Sally Scott's life and her inside thoughts at the moment, and the brand shop represents Sally Scott's bedroom and wardrobe. Her personality is expressed by furniture, books and accessories in the shop.

url www.sallyscott.com

Shanghai Tang

Shanghai Tang was founded in 1994 by Hong Kong businessman David Tang Wing-Cheung, with the mission to be the first global Chinese lifestyle brand. It does so by revitalizing Chinese designs, interweaving traditional Chinese culture with the dynamism of the 21st century. Unique to Shanghai Tang is Imperial Tailors, which revives the diminishing art of "Chinese haute couture" – delicately crafted apparel redelivered by a team of traditional Shanghainese tailors. Shanghai Tang's global network of 23 boutiques includes Shanghai, New York, Paris, London, Hong Kong and Singapore.

url www.shanghaitang.com

Shiseido

Shiseido was founded in 1872, four years after the Meiji Restoration. Arinobu Fukuhara, former head pharmacist to the Japanese navy, opened Japan's first private Western-style pharmacy in Ginza, the cultural and fashion hub of Japan, to introduce Western-style pharmaceuticals when herbal medicine was still mainstream. This avant-garde pharmacy, which was largely R&D-oriented, grew to become one of Japan's oldest surviving companies. Shiseido seeks to constantly advance the science of skincare, contributing to a beautiful and artful way of living.

url www.shiseido.co.jp

SUNDAY-VISION

Shinsuke Koshio founded SUNDAY-VISION in 1998, mainly creating graphic design and Web design in various fields. Works include textile design for UK apparel brand MACINTOSH, logo and Web design for the shop Parfumerie Generale in Paris, and Web design for Hikaru Utada.

url www.sunday-vision.com

Tsumori Chisato

Chief designer Tsumori Chisato renamed her label I.S. Chisato Tsumori Design in 1983. Her works have received many awards, including the prestigious Mainichi Fashion Grand Prix in 2002. Chisato chose Paris for her first fashion show outside Japan in 2003, leading to her international distribution in France, England, Italy and the U.S.

Uniqlo

Uniqlo designs, manufactures, markets and sells casual wear for everyone, providing people everywhere with the piece they need to create their own style – from T-shirts and sweaters to denim, outerwear and other trendy items. This concept has guided Uniqlo's actions since the establishment of its first store in 1984 in Hiroshima, Japan. Today Uniqlo has grown to over 760 stores worldwide.

url www.uniqlo.com

WABISABI

Wabisabi was founded by art directors and graphic designers Ryohey "wabi" Kudow and Kazushi "sabi" Nakanishi, in Japan in 1999. Their projects include advertising, small products and commercial films. Their original typeface "Hormone" won the silver prize in the 85th New York ADC, the bronze prize in the Taiwan International Poster Design Award 2006, and the gold prize in the International Triennial of Poster Design in Toyama in 2006.

url www.homeinc.jp

Young Kim

Suitman traveled six continents in search of unusual vernacular symbols, monuments and natural beauties. He likes to bring smiles to people everywhere. Besides his fine-art career, he and his partner Suitman work in advertising and marketing. Since 1998, they have been focusing their creative energy directing commercials. Clients include Nike, Adidas, Yohji Yamamoto, Sony, Sega, Blockbuster, Kodak, ESPN, and VH-1.

url www.suitman.org

ROCHAS